PIANO CHORD SONGBOOK

Gospel Hymns

ISBN 978-1-4950-3582-1

HAL•LEONARD® CORPORATION

7777 W. Bluemound Rd. P.O. Box 13819 Milwaukee, WI 53213

Copyright © 2015 by HAL LEONARD CORPORATION
International Copyright Secured All Rights Reserved

In Australia Contact:
Hal Leonard Australia Pty. Ltd.
4 Lentara Court
Cheltenham, Victoria, 3192 Australia
Email: ausadmin@halleonard.com.au

For all works contained herein:
Unauthorized copying, arranging, adapting, recording, Internet posting, public performance, or other distribution of the printed music in this publication is an infringement of copyright. Infringers are liable under the law.

Visit Hal Leonard Online at
www.halleonard.com

How to Use This Book

Piano Chord Songbooks include the lyrics and chords for each song. The melody of the first phrase of each song is also shown.

First, play the melody excerpt to get you started in the correct key. Then, sing the song, playing the chords that are shown above the lyrics.

Chords can be voiced in many different ways. For any chords that are unfamiliar, refer to the diagram that is provided for each chord. It shows the notes that you should play with your right hand. With your left hand, simply play the note that matches the name of the chord. For example, to play a C chord, play C-E-G in your right hand, and play a C in your left hand.

You will notice that some chords are *slash chords*; for example, C/G. With your right hand, play the chord that matches the note on the left side of the slash. With your left hand, play the note on the right side of the slash. So, to play a C/G chord, play a C chord (C-E-G) in your right hand, and play a G in your left hand.

Contents

4 Amazing Grace

6 Are You Washed in the Blood?

8 At Calvary

10 At the Cross

12 Blessed Assurance

14 Blessed Be the Name

16 Brighten the Corner Where You Are

18 Church in the Wildwood

20 Count Your Blessings

22 Does Jesus Care?

24 Down At the Cross (Glory to His Name)

26 Down by the Riverside

28 Dwelling in Beulah Land

32 The Eastern Gate

34 Footsteps of Jesus

31 Give Me That Old Time Religion

36 God Will Take Care of You

38 Hallelujah, We Shall Rise

40 He Hideth My Soul

42 He Keeps Me Singing

44 He's Got the Whole World in His Hands

46 Heavenly Sunlight

48 Higher Ground

50 His Eye Is on the Sparrow

52 I Feel Like Traveling On

56 I Have Decided to Follow Jesus

58 I Love to Tell the Story

60 I Must Tell Jesus

62 I Stand Amazed in the Presence (My Savior's Love)

64 I've Got Peace Like a River

66 In the Garden

68 Jesus Is the Sweetest Name I Know

70 Jesus Paid It All

72 Just a Closer Walk with Thee

74 Just As I Am

76 Just Over in the Gloryland

78 Leaning on the Everlasting Arms

53 Life's Railway to Heaven

80 The Lily of the Valley

82 Little Is Much When God Is in It

84 Love Lifted Me

86 The Love of God

88 My Savior First of All

90 Near the Cross

92 A New Name in Glory

94 No, Not One!

96 Nothing But the Blood

98 Oh, How I Love Jesus

100 The Old Rugged Cross

102 On Jordan's Stormy Banks

104 Pass Me Not, O Gentle Savior

106 Precious Memories

99 Revive Us Again

108 Rock of Ages

110 Send the Light

112 Shall We Gather at the River?

114 Since Jesus Came Into My Heart

116 Standing on the Promises

118 Sweet By and By

120 Sweet Hour of Prayer

122 Tell It to Jesus

113 There Is a Balm in Gilead

124 There Is a Fountain

130 There Is Power in the Blood

132 'Tis So Sweet to Trust in Jesus

134 Turn Your Eyes Upon Jesus

136 The Unclouded Day

138 Wayfaring Stranger

140 We'll Understand It Better By and By

142 What a Friend We Have in Jesus

127 When I Can Read My Title Clear

144 When the Roll Is Called Up Yonder

146 When the Saints Go Marching In

148 When We All Get to Heaven

150 Whispering Hope

152 Whiter Than Snow

154 Will the Circle Be Unbroken

155 Wonderful Grace of Jesus

158 Wonderful Peace

160 Wondrous Love

Amazing Grace

Words by John Newton
From *A Collection of Sacred Ballads*
Traditional American Melody
From Carrell and Clayton's *Virginia Harmony*
Arranged by Edwin O. Excell

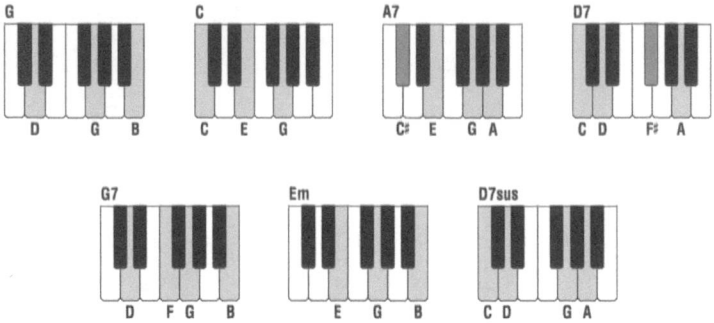

Verse 1

G C G
A - mazing grace, how sweet the sound,

A7 D7
That saved a wretch like me.

G G7/B C G
I once was lost but now am found,

Em D7 G
Was blind but now I see.

Verse 2

G C G
'Twas grace that taught my heart to fear,

A7 D7
And grace my fears re - lieved.

G G7/B C G
How precious did that grace ap - pear

Em D7 G
The hour I first be - lieved.

Copyright © 2015 by HAL LEONARD CORPORATION
International Copyright Secured All Rights Reserved

Verse 3

G **C** **G**
The Lord has prom - ised good to me,

A7 **D7sus**
His word my hope se - cures.

D7 **G** **G7/B** **C** **G**
He will my shield and portion be

Em **G** **D7** **G**
As long as life en - dures.

Verse 4

G **C** **G**
Through many dangers, toils and snares,

A7 **D7**
I have al - ready come.

G **G7/B** **C** **G**
'Tis grace hath brought me safe thus far,

Em **D7** **G**
And grace will lead me home.

Verse 5

G **C** **G**
When we've been there ten thou - sand years,

A7 **D7**
Bright shining as the sun,

G **G7/B** **C** **G**
We've no less days to sing God's praise

Em **D7** **G**
Than when we'd first be - gun.

Are You Washed in the Blood?

Words and Music by
Elisha A. Hoffman

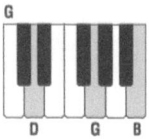

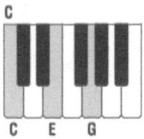

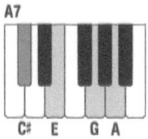

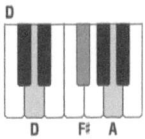

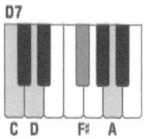

Verse 1

G **C/G** **G**
Have you been to Jesus for the cleans - ing power?

G **A7** **D**
Are you washed in the blood of the lamb?

G **C**
Are you fully trusting in His grace this hour?

G **D7** **G**
Are you washed in the blood of the Lamb?

Chorus 1

G **C**
Are you washed in the blood,

G **D** **G** **D**
In the soul cleans - ing blood of the Lamb?

D7 **G**
Are your garments spotless?

C
Are they white as snow?

G **D7** **G**
Are you washed in the blood of the Lamb?

Copyright © 2015 by HAL LEONARD CORPORATION
International Copyright Secured All Rights Reserved

Verse 2

G C/G G
Are you walking daily by the Sav - ior's side?

G A7 D
Are you washed in the blood of the Lamb?

G C
Do you rest each moment in the crucified?

G D7 G
Are you washed in the blood of the Lamb?

Chorus 2 *Repeat Chorus 1*

Verse 3

G C/G G
When the Bridegroom cometh will your robes be white?

G A7 D
Are you washed in the blood of the Lamb?

G C
Will your soul be ready for the mansions bright,

G D7 G
And be washed in the blood of the Lamb?

Chorus 3 *Repeat Chorus 1*

Verse 4

G C/G G
Lay a - side the garments that are stained with sin,

G A7 D
And be washed in the blood of the Lamb.

G C
There's a fountain flowing for the soul unclean,

G D7 G
O be washed in the blood of the lamb.

Chorus 4 *Repeat Chorus 1*

At Calvary

Words by William R. Newell
Music by Daniel B. Towner

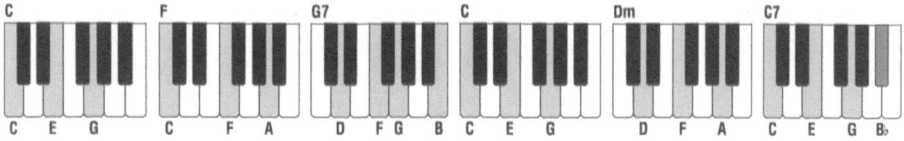

Verse 1

C **F/C** **C**
Years I spent in vanity and pride,

G7 **C** **F/C** **C**
Caring not my Lord was cru - ci - fied,

F/C **C** **C/E** **Dm/F** **G7** **C**
Knowing not it was for me He died on Cal - va - ry.

Chorus 1

F **C**
Mercy there was great and grace was free,

G7 **C** **C7/E**
Pardon there was multi - plied to me.

F **C** **C/E** **Dm/F** **G7** **C**
There my burdened soul found lib - erty, at Cal - va - ry.

Copyright © 2015 by HAL LEONARD CORPORATION
International Copyright Secured All Rights Reserved

Verse 2

C **F/C** **C**
By God's Word at last my sin I learned,

G7 **C** **F/C** **C**
Then I trembled at the law I'd spurned,

F/C **C** **C/E** **Dm/F** **G7** **C**
Till my guilty soul implor - ing turned to Cal - va - ry.

Chorus 2 *Repeat Chorus 1*

Verse 3

C **F/C** **C**
Now I've giv'n to Jesus ev - 'ry - thing.

G7 **C** **F/C** **C**
Now I gladly own Him as my King.

F/C **C** **C/E** **Dm/F** **G7** **C**
Now my raptured soul can on - ly sing of Cal - va - ry.

Chorus 3 *Repeat Chorus 1*

Verse 4

C **F/C** **C**
O the love that true salva - tion's plan!

G7 **C** **F/C** **C**
O the grace that brought it down to man.

F/C **C** **C/E** **Dm/F** **G7** **C**
O the mighty gulf that God did span at Cal - va - ry.

Chorus 4 *Repeat Chorus 1*

At the Cross

Words by Isaac Watts and Ralph E. Hudson
Music by Ralph E. Hudson

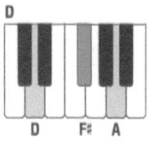

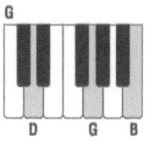

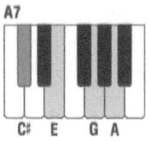

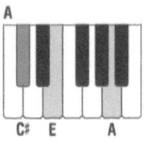

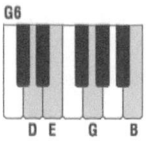

Verse 1

D
A - las! and did my Savior bleed?

D/F♯ G D/F♯ A7/E D A
And did my Sov - 'reign die?

D G/D D
Would He devote that sa - cred head

G6 D A7 D
For sinners such as I?

Chorus 1

D G/D D A
At the cross, at the cross where I first ___ saw the light,

A7 D
And the burden of my heart rolled a - way.

G D
It was there by faith I re - ceived my sight,

G6 A7 D
And now I am happy all the day!

Copyright © 2015 by HAL LEONARD CORPORATION
International Copyright Secured All Rights Reserved

Verse 2

D
Was it for crimes that I have done

D/F♯ G D/F♯ A7/E D A
He groaned up - on the tree?

D G/D D
Amazing pity, grace un - known!

G6 D A7 D
And love be - yond de - gree.

Chorus 2

Repeat Chorus 1

Verse 3

D
Well might the sun in darkness hide

D/F♯ G D/F♯ A7/E D A
And shut His glo - ries in,

D G/D D
When Christ, the mighty Mak - er, died

G6 D A7 D
For man, the crea - ture's sin.

Chorus 3

Repeat Chorus 1

Verse 4

D
But drops of grief can ne'er repay

D/F♯ G D/F♯ A7/E D A
The debt of love I owe.

D G/D D
Here, Lord, I give myself a - way,

G6 D A7 D
'Tis all that I can do!

Chorus 4

Repeat Chorus 1

Blessed Assurance

Lyrics by Fanny J. Crosby
Music by Phoebe Palmer Knapp

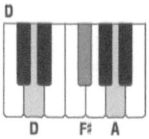

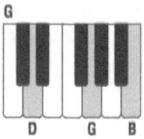

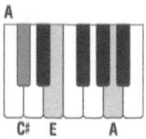

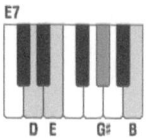

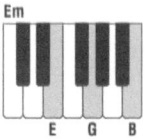

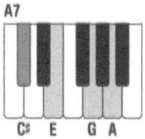

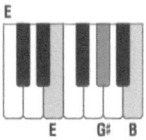

Verse 1

D G D
Blessed as - surance, Jesus is mine!

A E7 A
Oh, what a fore - taste of glory di - vine!

D G D
Heir of salvation, purchase of God,

G Em/G D A7 D
Born of His Spir - it, washed in His blood.

Chorus 1

D G D
This is my story, this is my song,

G D/F♯ A E A
Praising my Sav - ior all the day long.

A7 D G D
This is my story, this is my song,

G Em/G D A7 D
Praising my Sav - ior all the day long.

Copyright © 2015 by HAL LEONARD CORPORATION
International Copyright Secured All Rights Reserved

Verse 2

D G D
Perfect sub - mission, perfect de - light!

A E7 A
Visions of rap - ture now burst on my sight.

D G D
Angels descending bring from a - bove

G Em/G D A7 D
Echoes of mer - cy, whis - pers of love.

Chorus 2

Repeat Chorus 1

Verse 3

D G D
Perfect sub - mission, all is at rest,

A E7 A
I in my Sav - ior am happy and blessed.

D G D
Watching and waiting, looking a - bove,

G Em/G D A7 D
Filled with His good - ness, lost in His love.

Chorus 3

Repeat Chorus 1

Blessed Be the Name

Words by Charles Wesley
and Ralph E. Hudson
Traditional
Arranged by Ralph E. Hudson
and William J. Kirkpatrick

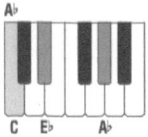

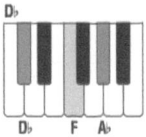

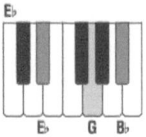

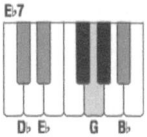

Verse 1

A♭ D♭ A♭
O for a thousand tongues to sing,
E♭
Blessed by the name of the Lord!
A♭ D♭ A♭
The glories of my God and King,
E♭7 A♭
Blessed be the name of the Lord!

Chorus 1

A♭ D♭ A♭
Blessed be the name! Blessed be the name!
E♭
Blessed be the name of the Lord!
A♭ D♭ A♭
Blessed be the name! Blessed be the name!
E♭ E♭7 A♭
Blessed be the name of the Lord!

Copyright © 2015 by HAL LEONARD CORPORATION
International Copyright Secured All Rights Reserved

Verse 2

A♭ D♭ A♭
Je - sus, the name that charms our fears,
E♭
Blessed be the name of the Lord!
A♭ D♭ A♭
'Tis music in the sinner's ears,
E♭7 A♭
Blessed be the name of the Lord!

Chorus 2

Repeat Chorus 1

Verse 3

A♭ D♭ A♭
He breaks the power of canceled sin,
E♭
Blessed be the name of the Lord!
A♭ D♭ A♭
His blood can make the foulest clean,
E♭7 A♭
Blessed be the name of the Lord!

Chorus 3

Repeat Chorus 1

Brighten the Corner Where You Are

Words by Ina Duley Ogdon
Music by Charles H. Gabriel

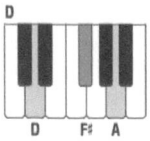

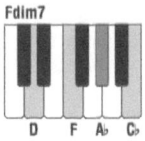

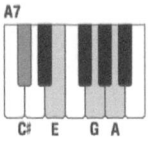

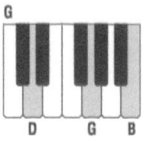

Verse 1

D **D/F♯** **Fdim7** **A7/E**
Do not wait until some deed of greatness you may do,

A7 **D**
Do not wait to shed your light a - far.

A7 **D** **G**
To the many duties ever near you now be true.

D **A7** **D**
Brighten the corner where you are.

Chorus 1

A7
Brighten the corner where you are.

D
Brighten the corner where you are.

G
Someone far from harbor you may guide across the bar.

D **A7** **D**
Brighten the corner where you are.

Copyright © 2015 by HAL LEONARD CORPORATION
International Copyright Secured All Rights Reserved

Verse 2

D **D/F♯** **Fdim7** **A7/E**
Just a - bove are clouded skies that you may help to clear.

A7 **D**
Let not narrow self your way de - bar,

A7 **D** **G**
Though in - to one heart alone may fall your song of cheer.

D **A7** **D**
Brighten the corner where you are.

Chorus 2 *Repeat Chorus 1*

Verse 3

D **D/F♯** **Fdim7** **A7/E**
Here for all your talent you may surely find a need.

A7 **D**
Here re - flect the Bright and Morning Star.

A7 **D** **G**
Even from your humble hand the bread of life may feed.

D **A7** **D**
Brighten the corner where you are.

Chorus 3 *Repeat Chorus 1*

Church in the Wildwood

Words and Music by
Dr. William S. Pitts

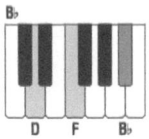

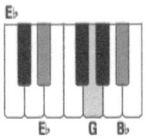

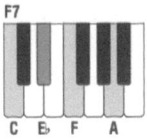

Verse 1

B♭ E♭B♭ F7
There's a church in the valley by the wild - wood,
B♭
No lovelier spot in the dale.
B♭/D E♭ B♭
No place is so dear to my childhood
F7 B♭
As the little brown church in the vale.

Chorus 1

B♭
Oh, come, come, come, come.
E♭B♭ F7
Come to the church in the wild - wood,
B♭
Oh, come to the church in the vale.
B♭/D E♭ B♭
No spot is so dear to my childhood
F7 B♭
As the little brown church in the vale.

Copyright © 2015 by HAL LEONARD CORPORATION
International Copyright Secured All Rights Reserved

Verse 2

B♭ E♭ B♭ F7
Oh, come to the church in the wild - wood,

B♭
To the trees where the wild flowers bloom,

B♭/D E♭ B♭
Where the parting hymn will be chanted,

F7 B♭
We will weep by the side of the tomb.

Chorus 2 *Repeat Chorus 1*

Verse 3

B♭ E♭ B♭ F7
From the church in the valley by the wild - wood,

B♭
When day fades away into night,

B♭/D E♭ B♭
I would fain from this spot of my childhood

F7 B♭
Wing my way to the mansions of light.

Chorus 3 *Repeat Chorus 1*

Count Your Blessings

Words by Johnson Oatman, Jr.
Music by Edwin O. Excell

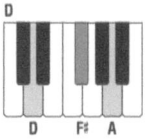

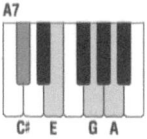

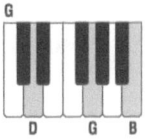

Verse 1

D **A7**
When upon life's billows you are tempest tossed,

D
When you are discouraged, thinking all is lost,

A7
Count your many blessings, name them one by one,

D A7 D
And it will surprise you what the Lord hath done.

Chorus 1

D **A7**
Count your blessings, name them one by one.

D
Count your blessings, see what God hath done.

G A7 G/A A7
Count your blessings, name them one by one.

D G D A7 D
Count your many blessings, see what God hath done.

Copyright © 2015 by HAL LEONARD CORPORATION
International Copyright Secured All Rights Reserved

Verse 2

D **A7**
Are you ever burdened with a load of care?

D
Does the cross seem heavy you are called to bear?

A7
Count your many blessings, ev'ry doubt will fly,

D A7 D
And you will be singing as the days go by.

Chorus 2 *Repeat Chorus 1*

Verse 3

D **A7**
When you look at others with their lands and gold,

D
Think that Christ has promised you His wealth untold.

A7
Count your many blessings, money cannot buy

D A7 D
Your reward in heaven nor your home on high.

Chorus 3 *Repeat Chorus 1*

Verse 4

D **A7**
So amid the conflict, whether great or small,

D
Do not be discouraged, God is over all.

A7
Count your many blessings, angels will attend,

D A7 D
Help and comfort give you to your jour - ney's end.

Chorus 4 *Repeat Chorus 1*

Does Jesus Care?

Words by Frank E. Graeff
Music by J. Lincoln Hall

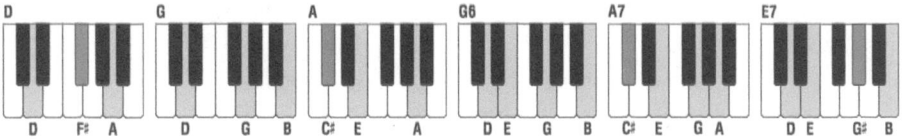

Verse 1

D G/D D G/D D
Does Jesus care when my heart is pained

A D
Too deeply for mirth and song;

G6
As the burdens press, and the cares distress,

D A7 D
And the way grows weary and long?

Chorus 1

A7 D
O yes, He cares, I know He cares.

A E7 A D A7
His heart is touched with my grief.

D G6
When the days are weary, the long nights dreary,

D A7 D G/D D
I know my Savior cares.

Copyright © 2015 by HAL LEONARD CORPORATION
International Copyright Secured All Rights Reserved

Verse 2

D G/D D G/D D
Does Jesus care when my way is dark

A D
With a nameless dread and fear?

G6
As the daylight fades into deep nightshades,

D A7 D
Does He care e - nough to be near?

Chorus 2 *Repeat Chorus 1*

Verse 3

D G/D D G/D D
Does Jesus care when I've tried and failed

A D
To re - sist some temptation strong;

G6
When for my deep grief I find no relief,

D A7 D
Though my tears flow all the night long?

Chorus 3 *Repeat Chorus 1*

Verse 4

D G/D D G/D D
Does Jesus care when I've said good - bye

A D
To the dearest on earth to me,

G6
And my sad heart aches till it nearly breaks;

D A7 D
Is it aught to Him? Does He see?

Chorus 4 *Repeat Chorus 1*

Down At the Cross

(Glory to His Name)

Words by Elisha A. Hoffman
Music by John H. Stockton

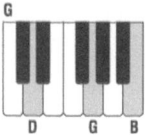

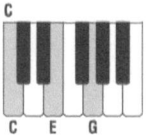

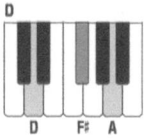

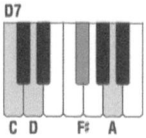

Verse 1

G G/B C G
Down at the cross where my Sav - ior died,

D
Down where for cleansing from sin I cried,

G G/B C G
There to my heart was the blood ap - plied;

G/D D7 G
Glory to His name!

Chorus 1

C G
Glory to His name!

D
Glory to His name!

G G/B C G
There to my heart was the blood ap - plied.

D7 G
Glory to His name.

Copyright © 2015 by HAL LEONARD CORPORATION
International Copyright Secured All Rights Reserved

Verse 2

G G/B C G
I am so won - drously saved from sin,

D
Jesus so sweetly abides with - in;

G G/B C G
There at the cross where He took me in;

G/D D7 G
Glory to His name!

Chorus 2 *Repeat Chorus 1*

Verse 3

G G/B C G
O precious foun - tain that saves from sin,

D
I am so glad that I entered in;

G G/B C G
There Jesus saves me and keeps me clean;

G/D D7 G
Glory to His name!

Chorus 3 *Repeat Chorus 1*

Verse 4

G G/B C G
Come to this foun - tain so rich and sweet;

D
Cast thy poor soul at the Savior's feet;

G G/B C G
Plunge in today and be made com - plete;

G/D D7 G
Glory to His name!

Chorus 4 *Repeat Chorus 1*

Down by the Riverside

African-American Spiritual

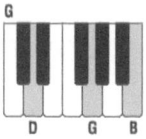

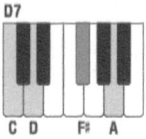

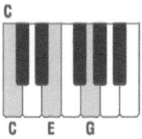

Verse 1

G
Gonna lay down my burden
D7
Down by the riverside,
G
Down by the riverside,

Down by the riverside.

Gonna lay down my burden

Down by the riverside
D7 **G**
And study war no more.

Chorus 1

C
I ain't gonna study war no more,
G
I ain't gonna study war no more,
D7 **G**
I ain't gonna study war no more.
C
I ain't gonna study war no more,
G
I ain't gonna study war no more,
D7 **G**
I ain't gonna study war no more.

Copyright © 2015 by HAL LEONARD CORPORATION
International Copyright Secured All Rights Reserved

Verse 2

G
Gonna lay down my sword and shield
D7
Down by the riverside,
G
Down by the riverside,

Down by the riverside.

Gonna lay down my sword and shield

Down by the riverside
D7 **G**
And study war no more.

Chorus 2 *Repeat Chorus 1*

Verse 3

G
Gonna try on my long white robe
D7
Down by the riverside,
G
Down by the riverside,

Down by the riverside.

Gonna try on my long white robe

Down by the riverside
D7 **G**
And study war no more.

Chorus 3 *Repeat Chorus 1*

Dwelling in Beulah Land

Words and Music by
C. Austin Miles

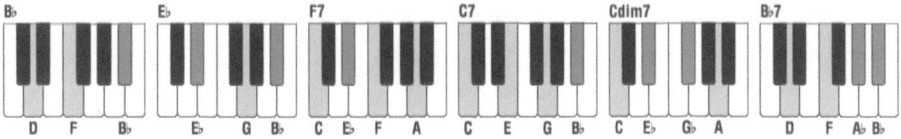

Verse 1

B♭ E♭ B♭ E♭ B♭
Far away the noise of strife

F7 B♭
Upon my ear is falling.

E♭ B♭ C7 F7
Then I know the sins of earth be - set on ev'ry hand.

B♭ E♭ B♭ E♭ B♭
Doubt and fear and things of earth

F7 B♭
In vain to me are calling.

E♭ B♭/D E♭ B♭ F7 B♭
None of these shall move me from Beu - lah Land.

Chorus 1

B♭ E♭ B♭ C°7 F7/C
I'm living on the mountain, underneath a cloudless sky.

F7 B♭ C7 F7
I'm drinking at the fountain that never shall run dry.

B♭ B♭7 E♭ B♭
O yes, I'm feasting on the manna from a bountiful sup - ply,

E♭ B♭ F7 B♭
For I am dwelling in Beu - lah Land.

Copyright © 2015 by HAL LEONARD CORPORATION
International Copyright Secured All Rights Reserved

Verse 2

B♭ E♭ B♭ E♭ B♭
Far below the storm of doubt

F7 B♭
Upon the world is beating.

E♭ B♭ C7 F7
Sons of men in battle long the enemy with - stand.

B♭ E♭ B♭ E♭ B♭
Safe am I with - in the castle

F7 B♭
Of God's Word re - treating,

E♭ B♭/D E♭ B♭ F7 B♭
Nothing then can reach me; 'tis Beu - lah Land.

Chorus 2 *Repeat Chorus 1*

Verse 3

B♭ E♭ B♭ E♭ B♭
Let the storm - y breez - es blow,

F7 B♭
Their cry can - not a - larm me.

E♭ B♭ C7 F7
I am safely sheltered here, pro - tected by God's hand.

B♭ E♭ B♭ E♭ B♭
Here the sun is al - ways shining,

F7 B♭
Here there's naught can harm me.

E♭ B♭/D E♭ B♭ F7 B♭
I am safe for - ever in Beu - lah Land.

Chorus 3 *Repeat Chorus 1*

Verse 4

B♭ E♭ B♭ E♭ B♭
Viewing here the works of God,

F7 B♭
I sink in contem - plation.

E♭ B♭ C7 F7
Hearing now His blessed voice, I see the way He planned.

B♭ E♭ B♭ E♭
Dwelling in the Spir - it,

B♭ F7 B♭
Here I learn of full sal - vation,

E♭ B♭/D E♭ B♭ F7 B♭
Gladly will I tarry in Beu - lah Land.

Chorus 4 *Repeat Chorus 1*

Give Me That Old Time Religion

Traditional

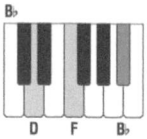

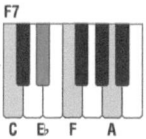

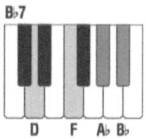

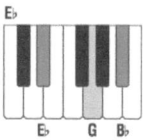

Verse 1

B♭
Give me that old time religion,

F7 **B♭**
Give me that old time re - ligion,

B♭7 **E♭**
Give me that old time re - ligion,

B♭ **F7** **B♭**
It's good e - nough for me.

Verse 2

B♭
It was good for our fathers,

F7 **B♭**
It was good for our fathers,

B♭7 **E♭**
It was good for our fathers,

B♭ **F7** **B♭**
And it's good e - nough for me.

Verse 3

B♭
It was good for our mothers,

F7 **B♭**
It was good for our mothers,

B♭7 **E♭**
It was good for our mothers,

B♭ **F7** **B♭**
And it's good e - nough for me.

Verse 4

Repeat Verse 1

Copyright © 2015 by HAL LEONARD CORPORATION
International Copyright Secured All Rights Reserved

The Eastern Gate

Words and Music by
Isaiah G. Martin

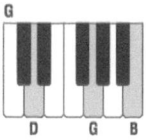

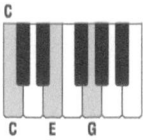

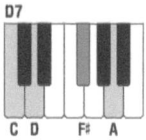

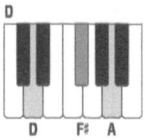

Verse 1

G **C** **G**
I will meet you in the morning, just inside the Eastern Gate;

C **D7** **G**
Then be ready, faithful pilgrim, lest with you it be too late.

Chorus 1

G
I will meet you in the morning, I will meet you in the morning,

D
Just inside the Eastern Gate over there.

G
I will meet you in the morning, I will meet you in the morning,

D7 **G**
I will meet you in the morning over there.

Copyright © 2015 by HAL LEONARD CORPORATION
International Copyright Secured All Rights Reserved

Verse 2

G C G
If you hasten off to glory, linger near the Eastern Gate;

C D7 G
For I'm coming in the morning, so you'll not have long to wait.

Chorus 2 *Repeat Chorus 1*

Verse 3

G
Keep your lamps all trimmed and burning,

C G
For the Bridegroom watch and wait.

C D7 G
He'll be with us at the meeting, just inside the Eastern Gate!

Chorus 3 *Repeat Chorus 1*

Verse 4

G C G
O the joy of that glad meeting with the saints who for us wait!

C D7 G
What a blessed happy meeting, just inside the Eastern Gate!

Chorus 4 *Repeat Chorus 1*

Footsteps of Jesus

Words by Mary B.C. Slade
Music by Asa B. Everett

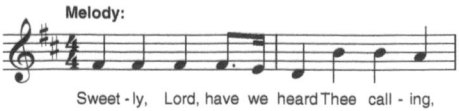

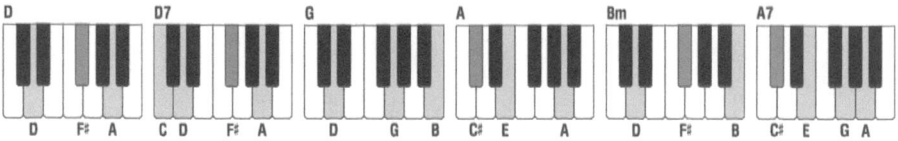

Verse 1

D D7 G D
Sweetly, Lord, have we heard Thee call - ing,

A
"Come, follow Me!"

D D7 G D
And we see where Thy footprints fall - ing

Bm D A7 D
Lead us to Thee.

Chorus 1

G D G/D D A
Footprints of Je - sus, that make the pathway glow.

D D7 G D
We will fol - low the steps of Je - sus

Bm D A7 D
Wher - e'er they go.

Copyright © 2015 by HAL LEONARD CORPORATION
International Copyright Secured All Rights Reserved

Verse 2

D D7 G D
Though the lead o'er the cold, dark moun - tains,

A
Seeking His sheep,

D D7 G D
Or along by Si - loam's foun - tains,

Bm D A7 D
Help - ing the weak.

Chorus 2

Repeat Chorus 1

Verse 3

D D7 G D
If they lead through the temple ho - ly,

A
Preaching the Word,

D D7 G D
Or in homes of the poor and low - ly,

Bm D A7 D
Serv - ing the Lord.

Chorus 3

Repeat Chorus 1

Verse 4

D D7 G D
Then at last, when on high He sees us,

A
Our journey done,

D D7 G D
We will rest where the steps of Je - sus

Bm D A7 D
End at His throne.

Chorus 4

Repeat Chorus 1

God Will Take Care of You

Words by Civilla D. Martin
Music by W. Stillman Martin

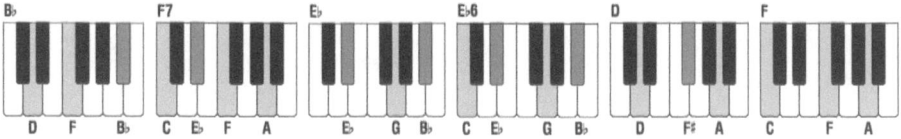

Verse 1

B♭ **F7 B♭**
Be not dismayed whate'er be - tide,

F7 **B♭**
God will take care of you.

F7 B♭
Beneath His wings of love a - bide,

F7 **B♭**
God will take care of you.

Chorus 1

E♭ **B♭**
God will take care of you,

F7 **B♭**
Through ev'ry day, o'er all the way.

B♭/D E♭6 D
He will take care of you,

E♭ **B♭ F B♭**
God will take care of you.

Copyright © 2015 by HAL LEONARD CORPORATION
International Copyright Secured All Rights Reserved

Verse 2

B♭ F7 B♭
Through days of toil when heart doth fail,

F7 B♭
God will take care of you.

F7 B♭
When dangers fierce your path as - sail,

F7 B♭
God will take care of you.

Chorus 2 *Repeat Chorus 1*

Verse 3

B♭ F7 B♭
All you may need He will pro - vide,

F7 B♭
God will take care of you.

F7 B♭
Nothing you ask will be de - nied,

F7 B♭
God will take care of you.

Chorus 3 *Repeat Chorus 1*

Verse 4

B♭ F7 B♭
No matter what may be the test,

F7 B♭
God will take care of you.

F7 B♭
Lean, weary one, upon His breast,

F7 B♭
God will take care of you.

Chorus 4 *Repeat Chorus 1*

Hallelujah, We Shall Rise

By J.E. Thomas

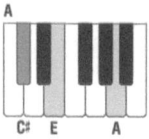

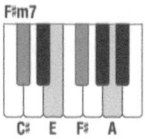

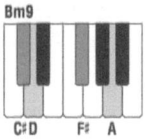

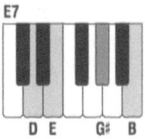

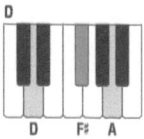

Verse 1

A
In the resurrection morning, when the trump of God shall sound,

F♯m7 B9 E7 A
(We shall rise.) Halle - lujah! We shall rise.

Then the saints will come rejoicing and no tears will e'er be found.

Chorus 1

A F♯m7 B9 E7 A
We shall rise, halle - lujah! In the morning, we shall rise.

(We shall rise.) Hallelujah! (We shall rise.) Amen.

D A
(We shall rise.) Hallelujah! In the resurrection morn - ing

When death's prison bars are broken,

F♯m7 B9 E7 A
We shall rise, halle - lujah! We shall rise.

Copyright © 2015 by HAL LEONARD CORPORATION
International Copyright Secured All Rights Reserved

A

Verse 2 In the resurrection morning, what a meeting it will be.

F♯m7 B9 E7 A

(We shall rise.) Halle - lujah! We shall rise!

When our fathers and our mothers and our loved ones we shall see.

Chorus 2 *Repeat Chorus 1*

A

Verse 3 In the resurrection morning, blessed thought it is to me.

F♯m7 B9 E7 A

(We shall rise.) Halle - lujah! We shall rise.

I shall see my blessed Savior, who so freely died for me.

Chorus 3 *Repeat Chorus 1*

A

Verse 4 In the resurrection morning, we shall meet Him in the air.

F♯m7 B9 E7 A

(We shall rise.) Halle - lujah! We shall rise.

And be carried up to glory, to our home so bright and fair.

Chorus 4 *Repeat Chorus 1*

He Hideth My Soul

Words by Fanny J. Crosby
Music by William J. Kirkpatrick

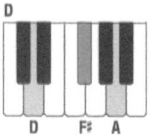

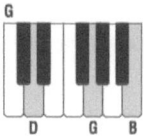

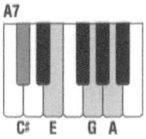

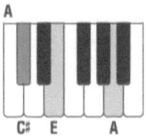

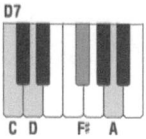

Verse 1

D **G** **D**
A wonderful Savior is Jesus, my Lord,

A7 D A
A wonderful Sav - ior to me.

A7 D **G**
He hideth my soul in the cleft of the rock,

D **A** **A7 D**
Where rivers of pleasure I see.

Chorus 1

A7 **D** **G/D D**
He hideth my soul in the cleft of the rock

A7 **A/C♯ D**
That shadows a dry, thirst - y land.

D7 G
He hideth my life in the depths of His love

D **A** **D** **A7 D A7 D**
And covers me there with His hand,

G D **A7** **D**
And covers me there with His hand.

Copyright © 2015 by HAL LEONARD CORPORATION
International Copyright Secured All Rights Reserved

Verse 2

D G D
A wonderful Savior is Jesus, my Lord.

A7 D A
He taketh my bur - den a - way.

A7 D G
He holdeth me up, and I shall not be moved,

D A A7 D
He giveth me strength as my day.

Chorus 2 *Repeat Chorus 1*

Verse 3

D G D
With numberless blessings each moment He crowns,

A7 D A
And filled with His full - ness di - vine,

A7 D G
I sing in my rapture, "O glory to God

D A A7 D
For such a Re - deemer as mine!"

Chorus 3 *Repeat Chorus 1*

Verse 4

D G D
When clothed in His brightness, trans - ported I rise

A7 D A
To meet Him in clouds of the sky,

A7 D G
His perfect salvation, His wonderful love,

D A A7 D
I'll shout with the millions on high.

Chorus 4 *Repeat Chorus 1*

He Keeps Me Singing

Words and Music by
Luther B. Bridgers

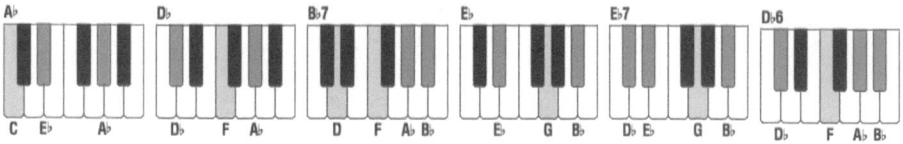

Verse 1

A♭ D♭ A♭ B♭7
There's within my heart a melody,

E♭ A♭ E♭7
Jesus whispers sweet and low:

A♭ D♭ A♭ B♭7
"Fear not, I am with thee, peace, be still,"

E♭ A♭ E♭7 A♭
In all of life's ebb and flow.

Chorus 1

A♭ A♭/C E♭7/B♭ E♭
Jesus, Je - sus, Je - sus,

A♭
Sweetest name I know.

A♭/C D♭6 D♭
Fills my ev - 'ry long - ing,

E♭ A♭ E♭7 A♭
Keeps me singing as I go.

Verse 2

A♭ D♭ A♭ B♭7
All my life was wrecked by sin and strife,

E♭ A♭ E♭7
Discord filled my heart with pain.

A♭ D♭ A♭ B♭7
Jesus swept a - cross the broken strings,

E♭ A♭ E♭7 A♭
Stirred the slumb'ring chords a - gain.

Chorus 2

Repeat Chorus 1

Copyright © 2015 by HAL LEONARD CORPORATION
International Copyright Secured All Rights Reserved

Verse 3

A♭ D♭ A♭ B♭7
Feasting on the rich - es of His grace,

E♭ A♭ E♭7
Resting 'neath His shelt'ring wing,

A♭ D♭ A♭ B♭7
Always looking on His smiling face,

E♭ A♭ E♭7 A♭
That is why I shout and sing.

Chorus 3 *Repeat Chorus 1*

Verse 4

A♭ D♭ A♭ B♭7
Though sometimes He leads through waters deep,

E♭ A♭ E♭7
Trials fall across the way,

A♭ D♭ A♭ B♭7
Though sometimes the path seems rough and steep,

E♭ A♭ E♭7 A♭
See His footprints all the way.

Chorus 4 *Repeat Chorus 1*

Verse 5

A♭ D♭ A♭ B♭7
Soon He's coming back to welcome me

E♭ A♭ E♭7
Far beyond the starry sky.

A♭ D♭ A♭ B♭7
I shall wing my flight to worlds unknown,

E♭ A♭ E♭7 A♭
I shall reign with Him on high.

Chorus 5 *Repeat Chorus 1*

He's Got the Whole World in His Hands

Traditional Spiritual

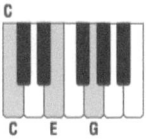

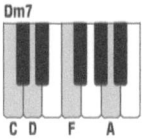

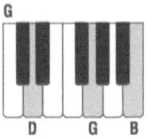

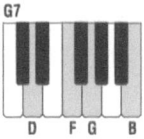

Chorus 1

C
He's got the whole world in His hands,

Dm7 G Dm7 G7
He's got the whole wide world in His hands,

C
He's got the whole world in His hands,

G7 C
He's got the whole world in His hands.

Verse 1

C
He's got the little tiny baby in His hands,

Dm7 G7 Dm7 G7
He's got the little tiny baby in His hands,

C
He's got the little tiny baby in His hands,

G7 C
He's got the whole world in His hands.

Chorus 2 *Repeat Chorus 1*

Copyright © 2010 by HAL LEONARD CORPORATION
International Copyright Secured All Rights Reserved

Verse 2

C
He's got you and me, brother, in His hands,
Dm7 G7 Dm7 G7
He's got you and me, sister, in His hands,
C
He's got you and me, brother, in His hands,
G7 C
He's got the whole world in His hands.

Chorus 3 *Repeat Chorus 1*

Verse 3

C
He's got ev'rybody here in His hands,
Dm7 G7 Dm7 G7
He's got ev'rybody here in His hands,
C
He's got ev'rybody here in His hands,
G7 C
He's got the whole world in His hands.

Chorus 4 *Repeat Chorus 1*

Heavenly Sunlight

Words by Henry J. Zelley
Music by George Harrison Cook

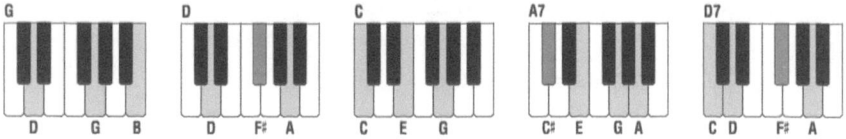

Verse 1

G D
Walking in sunlight all of my journey,

G C/G G A7 D
O - ver the mountains, through the deep vale;

G D
Jesus has said, "I'll never for - sake thee,"

G C/G G D7 G/D D7 G
Prom - ise divine that nev - er can fail.

Chorus 1

C C/E G/D C G
Heavenly sunlight, heav - en - ly sunlight,

A7 D
Flooding my soul with glory di - vine.

G D
Halle - lujah! I am re - joicing,

G C/G G D7 G/D D7 G
Sing - ing His praises, Je - sus is mine.

Copyright © 2015 by HAL LEONARD CORPORATION
International Copyright Secured All Rights Reserved

Verse 2

G D
Shadows a - round me, shadows a - bove me,

G C/G G A7 D
Nev - er conceal my Savior and Guide.

G D
He is the light, in Him is no darkness.

G C/G G D7 G/D D7 G
Ev - er I'm walking close to His side.

Chorus 2

Repeat Chorus 1

Verse 3

G D
In the bright sunlight, ever re - joicing,

G C/G G A7 D
Press - ing my way to mansions a - bove.

G D
Singing His praises, gladly I'm walking,

G C/G G D7 G/D D7 G
Walk - ing in sunlight, sun - light of love.

Chorus 3

Repeat Chorus 1

Higher Ground

Words by Johnson Oatman, Jr.
Music by Charles H. Gabriel

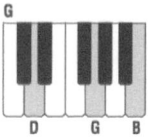

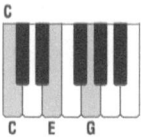

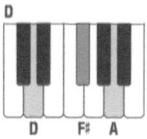

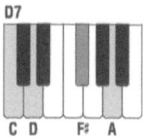

Verse 1

G C
I'm pressing on the upward way,

G D
New heights I'm gaining ev'ry day.

G C
Still praying as I'm onward bound,

G D7 G
"Lord, plant my feet on high - er ground."

Chorus 1

G D7
Lord, lift me up and let me stand,

G
By faith, on heaven's table - land,

D/A G/B C
A higher plane than I have found.

G D7 G
Lord, plant my feet on high - er ground.

Copyright © 2015 by HAL LEONARD CORPORATION
International Copyright Secured All Rights Reserved

Verse 2

G C
My heart has no desire to stay

G D
Where doubts a - rise and fears dis - may.

G C
Though some may dwell where these a - bound,

G D7 G
My prayer, my aim, is high - er ground.

Chorus 2 *Repeat Chorus 1*

Verse 3

G C
I want to live above the world,

G D
Though Satan's darts at me are hurled.

G C
For faith has caught the joyful sound,

G D7 G
The song of saints on high - er ground.

Chorus 3 *Repeat Chorus 1*

Verse 4

G C
I want to scale the utmost height,

G D
And catch a gleam of glory bright.

G C
But still I'll pray till heav'n I've found,

G D7 G
"Lord, lead me on to high - er ground."

Chorus 4 *Repeat Chorus 1*

His Eye Is on the Sparrow

Words by Civilla D. Martin
Music by Charles H. Gabriel

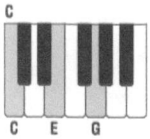

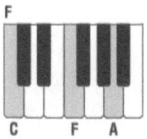

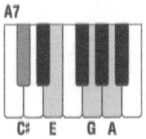

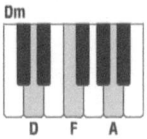

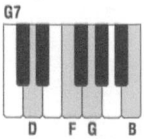

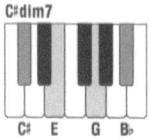

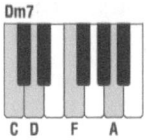

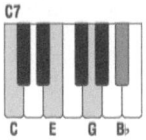

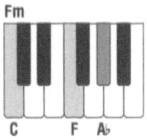

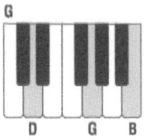

Verse 1

C
Why should I feel discouraged?
F C
Why should the shadows come?
A7 Dm
Why should my heart be lonely
G7 C
And long for heav'n and home

When Jesus is my portion?
G7 C F A7
My constant Friend is He.

Chorus 1

Dm G7 C
His eye is on the sparrow,
C♯dim7 Dm7 G7 C
And I know He watches me.
G7/D C/E C7 F
His eye is on the sparrow,
Fm C G7 C
And I know He watches me.
G C
I sing because I'm happy,
G C
I sing because I'm free.
C7/E F
For His eye is on the sparrow,
Fm C G7 C
And I know He watch - es me.

Copyright © 2015 by HAL LEONARD CORPORATION
International Copyright Secured All Rights Reserved

Verse 2

C
"Let not your heart be troubled,"

F **C**
His tender words I hear,

A7 **Dm**
And, resting on His goodness,

G7 **C**
I lose my doubt and fear.

Though by the path He leadeth

G7 **C** **F** **A7**
But one step I may see.

Chorus 2

Repeat Chorus 1

Verse 3

C
Whenever I am tempted,

F **C**
Whenever clouds a - rise,

A7 **Dm**
When songs give place to sighing,

G7 **C**
When hope within me dies,

I draw the closer to Him,

G7 **C** **F** **A7**
From care He sets me free.

Chorus 3

Repeat Chorus 1

I Feel Like Traveling On

Words by William Hunter
Traditional Melody
Music Arranged by James D. Vaughan

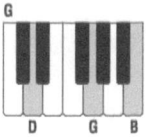

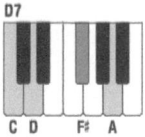

Verse 1

G D7
My heavenly home is bright and fair, I feel like traveling on.
G D7 G
No pain or death can enter there, I feel like traveling on.

Chorus 1

G
Yes, I feel like traveling on,
D7
I feel like traveling on.
G
My heavenly home is bright and fair,
D7 G
I feel like traveling on.

Verse 2

G D7
Its glitt'ring towers the sun outshine, I feel like traveling on.
G D7 G
That heav'nly mansion shall be mine, I feel like traveling on.

Chorus 2

Repeat Chorus 1

Verse 3

G D7
Let others seek a home below, I feel like traveling on.
G D7 G
Which flames devour or waves o'erflow, I feel like traveling on.

Chorus 3

Repeat Chorus 1

Verse 4

G D7
The Lord has been so good to me, I feel like traveling on.
G D7 G
Un - til that blessed home I see, I feel like traveling on.

Chorus 4

Repeat Chorus 1

Copyright © 2015 by HAL LEONARD CORPORATION
International Copyright Secured All Rights Reserved

Life's Railway to Heaven

Words by M.E. Abbey
Music by Charles D. Tillman

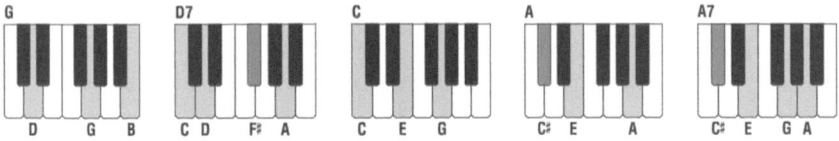

Verse 1

G D7 G
Life is like a mountain railroad,
C G
With an engineer that's brave.

We must make the run successful
A D7
From the cradle to the grave.
G D7 G
Watch the curves, the fills, the tunnels,
C G
Never falter, never quail.

Keep your hand upon the throttle,
G D7 G
And your eye up - on the rail.

Chorus 1

C G
Blessed Savior, Thou wilt guide us
A7 D7
Till we reach that blissful shore
G C
Where the angels wait to join us
G D7 G
In Thy praise for - ever - more.

Copyright © 2015 by HAL LEONARD CORPORATION
International Copyright Secured All Rights Reserved

Verse 2

G D7 G
You will roll up grades of trial,
C G
You will cross the bridge of strife.

See that Christ is your conductor
A D7
On this lightning train of life.
G D7 G
Always mindful of ob - struction,
C G
Do your duty, never fail.

Keep your hand upon the throttle,
G D7 G
And your eye up - on the rail.

Chorus 2

Repeat Chorus 1

Verse 3

G D7 G
You will often find ob - structions,
C G
Look for storms of wind and rain.

On a fill, or curve, or trestle
A D7
They will almost ditch your train.
G D7 G
Put your trust a - lone in Jesus,
C G
Never falter, never fail.

Keep your hand upon the throttle,
G D7 G
And your eye up - on the rail.

Chorus 3

Repeat Chorus 1

Verse 4

G D7 G
As you roll a - cross the trestle
C G
Spanning Jordan's swelling tide,

You behold the Union Depot
A D7
Into which your train will glide.
G D7 G
There you'll meet the Sup'rin - tendent,
C G
God the Father, God the Son.

With the hearty, joyous plaudit,
G D7 G
"Weary pilgrim, welcome home."

Chorus 4

Repeat Chorus 1

I Have Decided to Follow Jesus

Folk Melody from India
Arranged by Auila Read

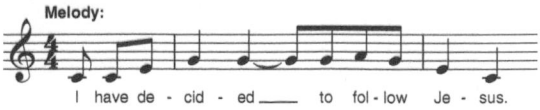

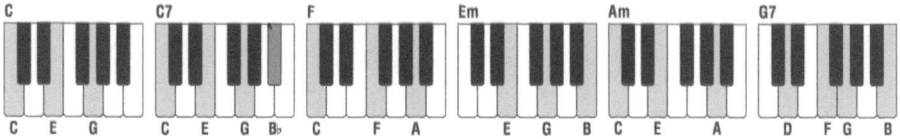

Verse 1

C
I have de - cided to follow Jesus.

C7 F C
I have de - cided to follow Je - sus.

Em Am
I have decided to follow Je - sus.

C G7 C
No turning back, no turning back.

Verse 2

C
The world be - hind me, the cross before me.

C7 F C
The world be - hind me, the cross before me.

Em Am
The world behind me, the cross be - fore me.

C G7 C
No turning back, no turning back.

Copyright © 2015 by HAL LEONARD CORPORATION
International Copyright Secured All Rights Reserved

Verse 3

C
Though none go with me, still I will follow.

C7 F C
Though none go with me, still I will fol - low.

Em Am
Though none go with me, still I will fol - low.

C G7 C
No turning back, no turning back.

Verse 4

C
Will you de - cide now to follow Jesus?

C7 F C
Will you de - cide now to follow Je - sus?

Em Am
Will you decide now to follow Je - sus?

C G7 C
No turning back, no turning back.

I Love to Tell the Story

Words by A. Catherine Hankey
Music by William G. Fischer

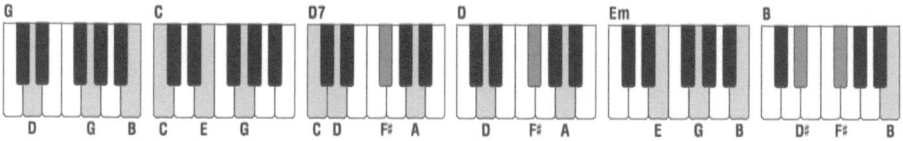

Verse 1

G G/B C G
I love to tell the story of unseen things a - bove,

D7 G G/B D
Of Jesus and His glo - ry, of Jesus and His love.

D/F♯ D7 G Em B
I love to tell the story be - cause I know 'tis true;

C G G/B D7 G/D D7 G
It satisfies my long - ings as noth - ing else can do.

Chorus 1

D7 G
I love to tell the sto - ry.

G/B C G
'Twill be my theme in glo - ry

G/B C
To tell the old, old sto - ry

G D7 G
Of Jesus and His love.

Copyright © 2015 by HAL LEONARD CORPORATION
International Copyright Secured All Rights Reserved

Verse 2

G G/B C G
I love to tell the story, more wonderful it seems

D7 G G/B D
Than all the golden fan - cies of all our gold - en dreams.

D/F♯ D7 G Em B
I love to tell the story, it did so much for me;

C G G/B D7 G/D D7 G
And that is just the rea - son I tell it now to thee.

Chorus 2 *Repeat Chorus 1*

Verse 3

G G/B C G
I love to tell the story, 'tis pleasant to re - peat

D7 G G/B D
What seems, each time I tell it, more wonderful - ly sweet.

D/F♯ D7 G Em B
I love to tell the story, for some have never heard

C G G/B D7 G/D D7 G
The message of salva - tion from God's own holy Word.

Chorus 3 *Repeat Chorus 1*

Verse 4

G G/B C G
I love to tell the story, for those who know it best

D7 G G/B D
Seem hungering and thirst - ing to hear it like the rest.

D/F♯ D7 G Em B
And when, in scenes of glory, I sing the new, new song,

C G G/B D7 G/D D7 G
'Twill be the old, old sto - ry that I have loved so long.

Chorus 4 *Repeat Chorus 1*

I Must Tell Jesus

Words and Music by
Elisha A. Hoffman

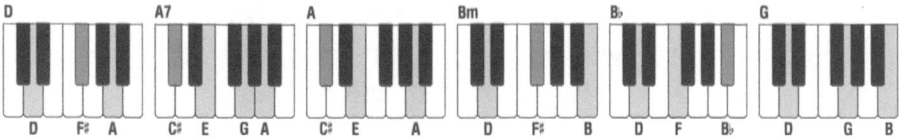

Verse 1

D **A7 D**
I must tell Jesus all of my tri - als;

A
I cannot bear these burdens a - lone.

D **A7 Bm**
In my distress He kindly will help me,

B♭ **D** **A7 D**
He ever loves and cares for His own.

Chorus 1

D **D/F♯** **G**
I must tell Jesus! I must tell Jesus!

D **A/C♯** **D A**
I cannot bear my burdens a - lone.

D **A7 Bm**
I must tell Jesus! I must tell Je - sus!

B♭ **D** **A7 D**
Jesus can help me, Jesus a - lone.

Copyright © 2015 by HAL LEONARD CORPORATION
International Copyright Secured All Rights Reserved

Verse 2

D **A7** **D**
I must tell Jesus all of my trou - bles;

A
He is a kind, compassionate Friend.

D **A7** **Bm**
If I but ask Him, He will de - liv - er,

B♭ **D** **A7** **D**
Make of my troubles quickly an end.

Chorus 2

Repeat Chorus 1

Verse 3

D **A7** **D**
O how the world to evil al - lures me!

A
O how my heart is tempted to sin!

D **A7** **Bm**
I must tell Jesus, and He will help me

B♭ **D** **A7** **D**
Over the world the vict'ry to win.

Chorus 3

Repeat Chorus 1

I Stand Amazed in the Presence

(My Savior's Love)

Words and Music by
Charles H. Gabriel

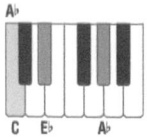

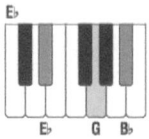

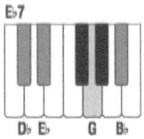

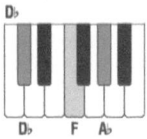

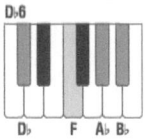

Verse 1

A♭ E♭
I stand amazed in the presence of Jesus,

A♭ E♭7 A♭
The Naz - a - rene,

D♭ A♭ A♭/C
And wonder how He could love me,

D♭6 A♭ E♭7 A♭
A sinner, con - demned, un - clean.

Chorus 1

A♭
How marvelous! How wonderful!

E♭
And my song shall ever be,

A♭
How marvelous! How wonderful

D♭6 A♭ E♭7 A♭
Is my Savior's love for me.

Verse 2

A♭ E♭
For me it was in the garden He prayed,

A♭ E♭7 A♭
"Not My will, but Thine."

D♭ A♭ A♭/C
He had no tears for His own griefs,

D♭6 A♭ E♭7 A♭
But sweat drops of blood for mine.

Chorus 2

Repeat Chorus 1

Copyright © 2015 by HAL LEONARD CORPORATION
International Copyright Secured All Rights Reserved

Verse 3

A♭
In pity angels beheld Him,
E♭ A♭ E♭7 A♭
And came from the world of light
D♭ A♭ A♭/C
To comfort Him in the sor - rows
D♭6 A♭ E♭7 A♭
He bore for my soul that night.

Chorus 3

Repeat Chorus 1

Verse 4

A♭
He took my sins and my sorrows,
E♭ A♭ E♭7 A♭
He made them His ver - y own.
D♭ A♭ A♭/C
He bore the burden to Cal - v'ry,
D♭6 A♭ E♭7 A♭
And suffered and died a - lone.

Chorus 4

Repeat Chorus 1

Verse 5

A♭
When with the ransomed in glory
E♭ A♭ E♭7 A♭
His face I at last shall see,
D♭ A♭ A♭/C
'Twill be my joy through the ag - es
D♭6 A♭ E♭7 A♭
To sing of His love for me.

Chorus 5

Repeat Chorus 1

I've Got Peace Like a River

Traditional

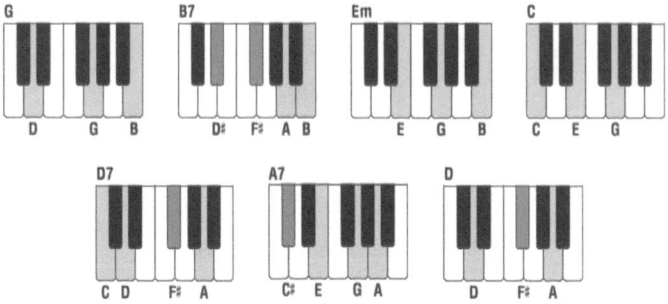

Verse 1

G
I've got peace like a river,

B7 Em C D7
I've got peace like a river,

G Em A7 D D7
I've got peace like a river in my soul;

G
I've got peace like a river,

B7 Em C D7
I've got peace like a river,

G Em A7 D7 G
I've got peace like a river in my soul.

Copyright © 2010 by HAL LEONARD CORPORATION
International Copyright Secured All Rights Reserved

Verse 2

G
I've got love like an ocean,

B7 Em C D7
I've got love like an ocean,

G Em A7 D D7
I've got love like an ocean in my soul;

G
I've got love like an ocean,

B7 Em C D7
I've got love like an ocean,

G Em A7 D7 G
I've got love like an ocean in my soul.

Verse 3

G
I've got joy like a fountain,

B7 Em C D7
I've got joy like a fountain,

G Em A7 D D7
I've got joy like a fountain in my soul;

G
I've got joy like a fountain,

B7 Em C D7
I've got joy like a fountain,

G Em A7 D7 G
I've got joy like a fountain in my soul.

In the Garden

Words and Music by
C. Austin Miles

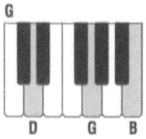

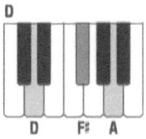

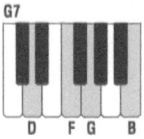

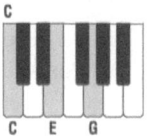

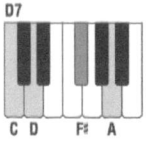

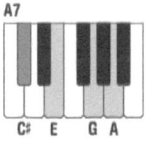

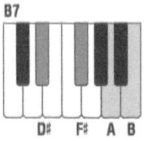

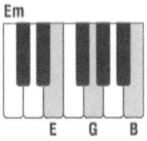

Verse 1

G **G/B** **D** **G**
I come to the gar - den a - lone,

G7/B **C** **G**
While the dew is still on the roses.

D7 **G/B** **D** **G**
And the voice I hear, falling on my ear,

A7 **D** **A7** **D7**
The Son of God dis - clos - es.

Chorus 1

G **D7**
And He walks with me, and He talks with me,

G
And He tells me I am His own.

B7 **Em** **G7/D** **C**
And the joy we share as we tar - ry there

G **D7** **G**
None other has ever known.

Copyright © 2015 by HAL LEONARD CORPORATION
International Copyright Secured All Rights Reserved

Verse 2

G **G/B D G**
He speaks, and the sound of His voice

G7/B C **G**
Is so sweet the birds hush their singing.

D7 **G/B D G**
And the melody that He gave to me

A7 **D A7 D7**
With - in my heart is ring - ing.

Chorus 2

Repeat Chorus 1

Verse 3

G **G/B D G**
I'd stay in the gar - den with Him

G7/B C **G**
Though the night around me be falling.

D7 **G/B D G**
But He bids me go; through the voice of woe,

A7 **D A7 D7**
His voice to me is call - ing.

Chorus 3

Repeat Chorus 1

Jesus Is the Sweetest Name I Know

Words and Music by
Lela Long

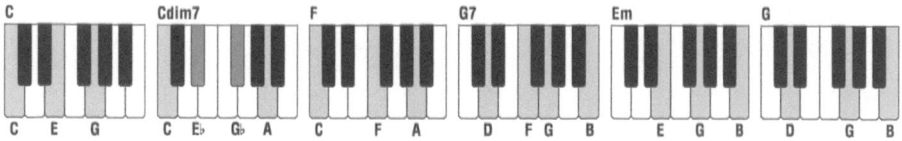

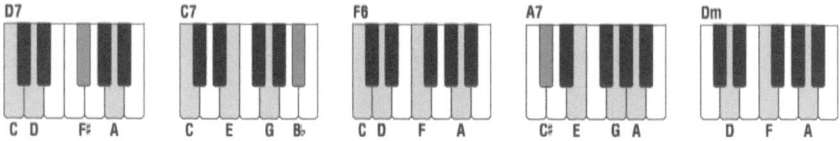

Verse 1

C Cdim7 C F C G7/F C/E
There have been names that I have loved to hear,

C Cdim7 C F G7 C
But never has there been a name so dear

G7 Em/G G7 Em/G G7
To this heart of mine

C F C
As the name divine,

G D7 G7
The precious, precious name of Je - sus.

Chorus 1

C Cdim7 C F C
Jesus is the sweetest name I know,

Em/G G7 F C
And He's just the same as His love - ly name.

Cdim7 C F C
And that's the rea - son why I love Him so,

C7 F6 A7 Dm G C
For Jesus is the sweetest name I know.

Copyright © 2015 by HAL LEONARD CORPORATION
International Copyright Secured All Rights Reserved

Verse 2

C Cdim7 C F C G7/F C/E
There is no name in earth or heav'n a - bove

C Cdim7 C F G7 C
That we should give such honor and such love

G7 Em/G G7 Em/G G7
As the bless - ed name.

C F C
Let us all acclaim

G D7 G7
That wondrous, glorious name of Je - sus.

Chorus 2

Repeat Chorus 1

Verse 3

C Cdim7 C F C G7/F C/E
And someday I shall see Him face to face

C Cdim7 C F G7 C
To thank and praise Him for His won - drous grace,

G7 Em/G G7 Em/G G7
Which He gave to me

C F C
When He made me free,

G D7 G7
The blessed Son of God called Je - sus.

Chorus 3

Repeat Chorus 1

Jesus Paid It All

Words by Elvina M. Hall
Music by John T. Grape

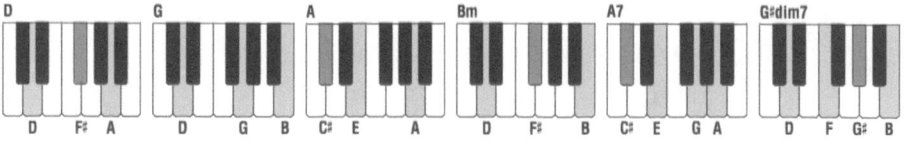

Verse 1

D G/D D
I hear the Savior say,

D/F♯ A Bm A D
"Thy strength in - deed is small.

G/D D
Child of weak - ness, watch and pray,

D/F♯ G D/A A7 D
Find in Me thine all in all."

Chorus 1

G/D D
Je - sus paid it all,

G/D D A
All to Him I owe.

D G/D D D/F♯ G
Sin had left a crim - son stain,

G♯°7 D/A A7 D
He washed it white as snow.

Copyright © 2015 by HAL LEONARD CORPORATION
International Copyright Secured All Rights Reserved

Verse 2

D G/D D
Lord, now in - deed I find

D/F♯ A Bm A D
Thy pow'r, and Thine a - lone,

G/D D
Can change the leper's spots

D/F♯ G D/A A7 D
And _____ melt the heart of stone.

Chorus 2

Repeat Chorus 1

Verse 3

D G/D D
For noth - ing good have I

D/F♯ A Bm A D
Where - by Thy grace to claim.

G/D D
I'll wash my garments white

D/F♯ G D/A A7 D
In the blood of Cal - v'ry's Lamb.

Chorus 3

Repeat Chorus 1

Verse 4

D G/D D
And when be - fore the throne

D/F♯ A Bm A D
I stand In Him com - plete,

G/D D
"Jesus died my soul to save,"

D/F♯ G D/A A7 D
My _____ lips shall still re - peat.

Chorus 4

Repeat Chorus 1

Just a Closer Walk with Thee

Traditional
Arranged by Kenneth Morris

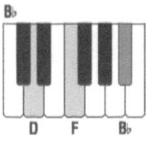

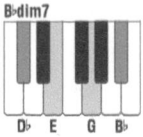

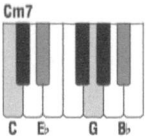

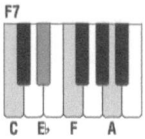

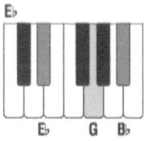

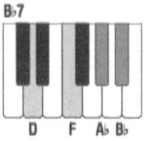

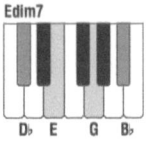

Verse 1

B♭ B♭dim7 Cm7 F7
I am weak but Thou art strong.

E♭/F B♭
Jesus, keep me from all wrong.

B♭7 E♭ Edim7
I'll be satisfied as long

B♭ F7 B♭
As I walk, let me walk close to Thee.

Chorus 1

B♭ B♭dim7 Cm7 F7
Just a closer walk with Thee,

E♭/F B♭
Grant it, Jesus, is my plea.

B♭7 E♭ Edim7
Daily walking close to Thee,

B♭ F7 B♭
Let it be, dear Lord, let it be.

Copyright © 2015 by HAL LEONARD CORPORATION
International Copyright Secured All Rights Reserved

Verse 2

B♭ B♭dim7 Cm7 F7
Through this world of toil and snares,

E♭/F B♭
If I falter, Lord, who cares?

B♭7 E♭ Edim7
Who with me my burden shares?

B♭ F7 B♭
None but Thee, dear Lord, none but Thee.

Chorus 2

Repeat Chorus 1

Verse 3

B♭ B♭dim7 Cm7 F7
When my feeble life is o'er,

E♭/F B♭
Time for me will be no more.

B♭7 E♭ Edim7
Guide me gently, safely o'er

B♭ F7 B♭
To Thy kingdom shore, to Thy shore.

Chorus 3

Repeat Chorus 1

Just As I Am

Words by Charlotte Elliott
Music by William B. Bradbury

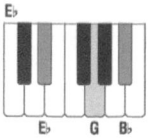

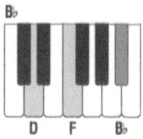

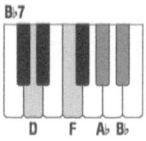

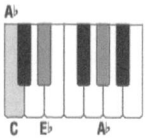

Verse 1

E♭ B♭ E♭
Just as I am, with - out one plea,
B♭ E♭/B♭ B♭7 A♭/E♭ E♭
But that Thy blood was shed for me,
A♭
And that Thou bidd'st me come to Thee,
E♭ B♭ E♭
O Lamb of God, I come! I come!

Verse 2

E♭ B♭ E♭
Just as I am, and waiting not
B♭ E♭/B♭ B♭7 A♭/E♭ E♭
To rid my soul of one dark blot,
A♭
To Thee whose blood can cleanse each spot,
E♭ B♭ E♭
O Lamb of God, I come! I come!

Copyright © 2015 by HAL LEONARD CORPORATION
International Copyright Secured All Rights Reserved

Verse 3

E♭ B♭ E♭
Just as I am, though tossed a - bout
B♭ E♭/B♭ B♭7 A♭/E♭ E♭
With many a conflict, many a doubt.
A♭
Fighting and fears with - in, without,
E♭ B♭ E♭
O Lamb of God, I come! I come!

Verse 4

E♭ B♭ E♭
Just as I am, poor, wretched, blind;
B♭ E♭/B♭ B♭7 A♭/E♭ E♭
Sight, rich - es, healing of the mind –
A♭
Yea, all I need in Thee to find,
E♭ B♭ E♭
O Lamb of God, I come! I come!

Verse 5

E♭ B♭ E♭
Just as I am, Thou wilt re - ceive,
B♭ E♭/B♭ B♭7 A♭/E♭ E♭
Wilt wel - come, pardon, cleanse, relieve.
A♭
Because Thy promise I believe,
E♭ B♭ E♭
O Lamb of God, I come! I come!

Verse 6

E♭ B♭ E♭
Just as I am, Thy love un - known
B♭ E♭/B♭ B♭7 A♭/E♭ E♭
Hath bro - ken ev'ry bar - rier down.
A♭
Now to be Thine, yea, Thine alone,
E♭ B♭ E♭
O Lamb of God, I come! I come!

Just Over in the Gloryland

Words by James W. Acuff
Music by Emmett S. Dean

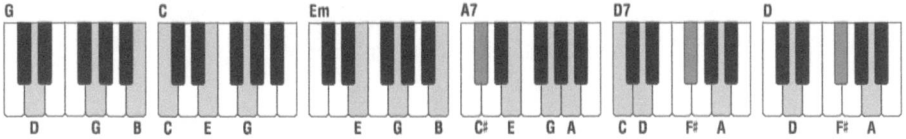

Verse 1

G C/G G C C/E G
I've a home pre - pared where the saints a - bide,

Em A7 D7
Just over in the glory - land.

G C/G G C C/E G
And I long to be by my Sav - ior's side,

Em G/D D7 G
Just over in the glo - ry - land.

Chorus 1

G D7 G
Just over in the gloryland

G/B C C/E G
I'll join the happy an - gel band,

Em A7 D A7
Just over in the glory - land.

D G D7 G
Just over in the gloryland,

G/B C G
There with the mighty host I'll stand,

Em G/D D7 G C/G G
Just over in the glo - ry - land.

Copyright © 2015 by HAL LEONARD CORPORATION
International Copyright Secured All Rights Reserved

Verse 2

G C/G G C C/E G
I am on my way to those man - sions fair,

Em A7 D7
Just over in the glory - land.

G C/G G C C/E G
There to sing God's praise and His glo - ry share,

Em G/D D7 G
Just over in the glo - ry - land.

Chorus 2

Repeat Chorus 1

Verse 3

G C/G G C C/E G
What a joy - ful thought that my Lord I'll see,

Em A7 D7
Just over in the glory - land.

G C/G G C C/E G
And with kin - dred saved, there for - ev - er be,

Em G/D D7 G
Just over in the glo - ry - land.

Chorus 3

Repeat Chorus 1

Verse 4

G C/G G C C/E G
With the blood - washed throng I will shout and sing,

Em A7 D7
Just over in the glory - land.

G C/G G C C/E G
Glad ho - san - nas to Christ, the Lord and King,

Em G/D D7 G
Just over in the glo - ry - land.

Chorus 4

Repeat Chorus 1

Leaning on the Everlasting Arms

Words by Elisha A. Hoffman
Music by Anthony J. Showalter

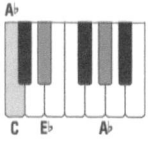

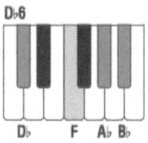

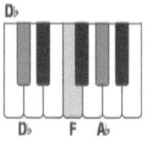

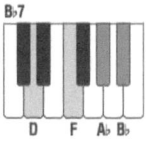

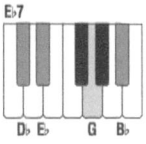

Verse 1

A♭ D♭6 D♭
What a fellowship, what a joy divine,
A♭ B♭7 E♭7
Leaning on the Ever - lasting Arms!
A♭ D♭6 D♭
What a blessedness, what a peace is mine,
A♭ E♭7 A♭
Leaning on the Everlast - ing Arms!

Chorus 1

A♭ D♭ A♭ B♭7 E♭
Leaning, leaning, safe and secure from all a - larms.
A♭ D♭ A♭ E♭7 A♭
Leaning, leaning, leaning on the Everlast - ing Arms!

Copyright © 2015 by HAL LEONARD CORPORATION
International Copyright Secured All Rights Reserved

Verse 2

A♭ D♭6 D♭
O how sweet to walk in this pilgrim way,

A♭ B♭7 E♭7
Leaning on the Ever - lasting Arms!

A♭ D♭6 D♭
O how bright the path grows from day to day,

A♭ E♭7 A♭
Leaning on the Everlast - ing Arms!

Chorus 2

Repeat Chorus 1

Verse 3

A♭ D♭6 D♭
What have I to dread, what have I to fear,

A♭ B♭7 E♭7
Leaning on the Ever - lasting Arms?

A♭ D♭6 D♭
I have blessed peace with my Lord so near,

A♭ E♭7 A♭
Leaning on the Everlast - ing Arms!

Chorus 3

Repeat Chorus 1

The Lily of the Valley

Words by Charles W. Fry
Music by William S. Hays

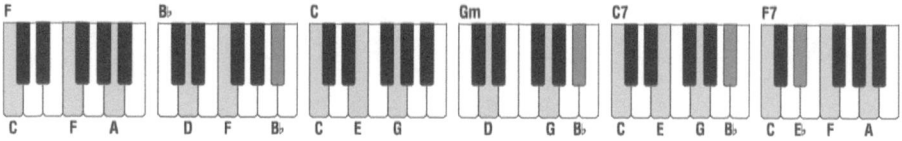

Verse 1

F B♭ F B♭ F
I have found a friend in Jesus, He's ev'rything to me.

B♭ F/A F C
He's the fairest of ten thou - sand to my soul.

F B♭ F B♭ F
The Lily of the Valley, in Him alone I see,

Gm/B♭ F C7 F
All I need to cleanse and make me ful - ly whole.

F7/A B♭ F
In sorrow He's my comfort, in trou - ble He's my stay,

B♭ F/A F C
He tells me ev'ry care on Him to roll.

Chorus 1

F B♭ F
He's the Lily of the Valley,

B♭ F
The Bright and Morning Star.

Gm/B♭ F C7 F
He's the fairest of ten thousand to my soul.

Copyright © 2015 by HAL LEONARD CORPORATION
International Copyright Secured All Rights Reserved

Verse 2

F B♭ F B♭ F
He all my griefs has taken, and all my sorrows borne.

B♭ F/A F C
In temptation He's my strong and might - y tow'r.

F B♭ F B♭ F
I have all for Him forsaken, and all my idols torn

Gm/B♭ F C7 F
From my heart, and now He keeps me by his pow'r.

F7/A B♭ F
Though all the world forsake me and Sa - tan tempt me sore,

B♭ F/A F C
Through Jesus I shall safe - ly reach the goal.

Chorus 2

Repeat Chorus 1

Verse 3

F B♭ F B♭ F
He will never, nev - er leave me, nor yet forsake me here,

B♭ F/A F C
While I live by faith and do His bless - ed will.

F B♭ F B♭ F
A wall of fire about me, I've nothing now to fear,

Gm/B♭ F C7 F
With His manna He my hungry soul shall fill.

F7/A B♭ F
Then sweeping up to glory I'll see His blessed face

B♭ F/A F C
Where rivers of de - light shall ev - er roll.

Chorus 3

Repeat Chorus 1

Little Is Much When God Is in It

Words by Mrs. F.W. Suffield
and Dwight Brock
Music by Mrs. F.W. Suffield

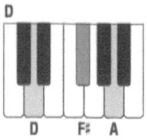

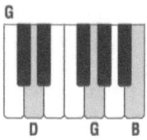

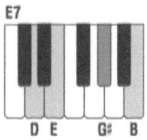

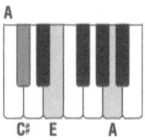

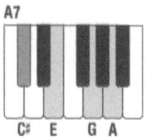

Verse 1

D
In the harvest field now ripened,

G D E7 A
There is work for all to do.

A7 D
Hark, the voice of God is calling,

G D A7 D
To the harvest call - ing you.

Chorus 1

D G/D D
Little is much when God is in it.

G/D D A
Labor not for wealth or fame.

A7 D
There's a crown, and you can win it

G D A7 D
If you go in Je - sus' name.

Copyright © 2015 by HAL LEONARD CORPORATION
International Copyright Secured All Rights Reserved

Verse 2

D
Does the place you're called to labor

G D E7 A
Seem so small and little - known?

A7 D
It is great if God is in it,

G D A7 D
And He'll not forget His own.

Chorus 2

Repeat Chorus 1

Verse 3

D
Are you laid aside from service,

G D E7 A
Body worn from toil and care?

A7 D
You can still be in the battle

G D A7 D
In the sacred place of prayer.

Chorus 3

Repeat Chorus 1

Verse 4

D
When the conflict here is ended

G D E7 A
And our race on earth is run,

A7 D
He will say, if we are faithful,

G D A7 D
"Welcome home, my child, well done."

Chorus 4

Repeat Chorus 1

Love Lifted Me

Words by James Rowe
Music by Howard E. Smith

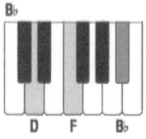

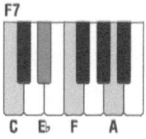

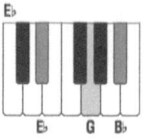

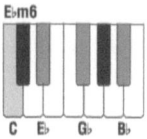

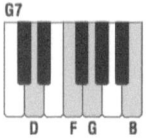

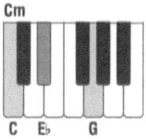

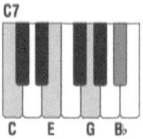

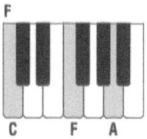

Verse 1

B♭ **F7**
I was sinking deep in sin, far from the peaceful shore,

B♭
Very deeply stained within, sinking to rise no more.

E♭
But the Master of the sea heard my despairing cry,

E♭m6 B♭ E♭ B♭ F7 B♭
From the wa - ters lifted me, now safe am I.

Chorus 1

F7 B♭ E♭/B♭ B♭ E♭ G7/D Cm
Love lifted me! _____ Love lifted me!

E♭ B♭ C7 F F7
When nothing else could help, love lifted me.

B♭ F7 B♭ E♭/B♭ B♭ E♭ G7/D Cm
Love lifted me! _____ Love lifted me!

E♭ B♭ F7 B♭
When nothing else could help, love lift - ed me.

Copyright © 2015 by HAL LEONARD CORPORATION
International Copyright Secured All Rights Reserved

Verse 2

B♭ **F7**
All my heart to Him I give, ever to Him I'll cling,

B♭
In His blessed presence live, ever His praises sing.

E♭
Love so mighty and so true merits my soul's best songs;

E♭m6 **B♭** **E♭** **B♭** **F7** **B♭**
Faithful lov - ing service, too, to Him be - longs.

Chorus 2 *Repeat Chorus 1*

Verse 3

B♭ **F7**
Souls in danger, look above, Jesus completely saves.

B♭
He will lift you, by His love, out of the angry waves.

E♭
He's the Master of the sea, billows His will o - bey.

E♭m6 **B♭** **E♭** **B♭** **F7** **B♭**
He your Sav - ior wants to be; be saved to - day.

Chorus 3 *Repeat Chorus 1*

The Love of God

Words and Music by
Frederick M. Lehman

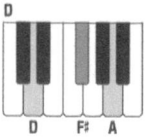

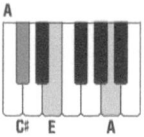

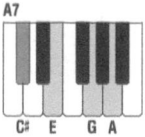

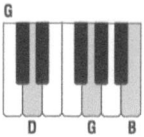

Verse 1

D **A** **D**
The love of God is greater far than tongue or pen can ever tell.

A7 **D**
It goes beyond the highest star, and reaches to the lowest hell.

G **D** **A** **A7** **D**
The guilty pair, bowed down with care, God gave His Son to win.

G **D** **A7** **D**
His erring child He recon - ciled, and pardoned from his sin.

Chorus 1

D **G** **D**
O love of God, how rich and pure!

A **D**
How measure - less and strong!

G **D**
It shall for - evermore en - dure –

A7 **D**
The saints' and angels' song.

Copyright © 2015 by HAL LEONARD CORPORATION
International Copyright Secured All Rights Reserved

Verse 2

D A D
When hoary time shall pass away, and earthly thrones and kingdoms fall,

A7 D
When men who here refuse to pray, on rocks and hills and mountains call.

G D A A7 D
God's love, so sure, shall still en - dure, all measure - less and strong.

G D A7 D
Redeeming grace to Adam's race – the saints' and angels' song.

Chorus 2 *Repeat Chorus 1*

Verse 3

D A D
Could we with ink the ocean fill, and were the skies of parchment made,

A7 D
Were ev'ry stalk on earth a quill, and ev'ry man a scribe by trade,

G D A A7 D
To write the love of God a - bove would drain the o - cean dry.

G D A7 D
Nor could the scroll contain the whole, though stretched from sky to sky.

Chorus 3 *Repeat Chorus 1*

My Savior First of All

Words by Fanny J. Crosby
Music by John R. Sweney

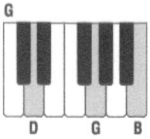

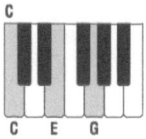

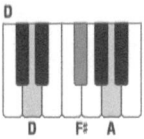

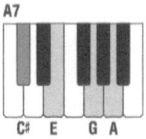

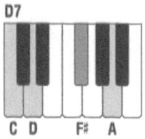

Verse 1

G **C** **G**
When my lifework is ended and I cross the swelling tide,

D/F♯ **A7/E** **D**
When the bright and glorious morning I shall see,

G **G/B** **C**
I shall know my Redeemer when I reach the other side,

G **D7** **C/D** **D7** **G**
And His smile will be the first to wel - come me.

Chorus 1

D7 **C/D** **D7** **G**
I shall know Him, I shall know Him,

D7/A **G** **D/F♯** **A7/E** **D**
And redeemed by His side ____ I shall stand.

G/D **D7** **G** **C/G** **G** **C**
I shall know Him, I shall know Him

G **D** **C/D** **D7** **G**
By the prints of the nails in His hand.

Copyright © 2015 by HAL LEONARD CORPORATION
International Copyright Secured All Rights Reserved

Verse 2

G C G
O the soul-thrilling rapture when I view His blessed face,

D/F♯ A7/E D
And the luster of His kindly beam - ing eye.

G G/B C
How my full heart will praise Him for the mercy, love, and grace

G D7 C/D D7 G
That pre - pare for me a mansion in the sky.

Chorus 2 *Repeat Chorus 1*

Verse 3

G C G
O the dear ones in glory, how they beckon me to come,

D/F♯ A7/E D
And our parting at the river I re - call.

G G/B C
To the sweet vales of Eden they will sing my welcome home,

G D7 C/D D7 G
But I long to meet my Savior first of all.

Chorus 3 *Repeat Chorus 1*

Verse 4

G C G
Through the gates to the city, in a robe of spotless white,

D/F♯ A7/E D
He will lead me where no tears will ev - er fall.

G G/B C
In the glad song of ages I shall mingle with delight,

G D7 C/D D7 G
But I long to meet my Savior first of all.

Chorus 4 *Repeat Chorus 1*

Near the Cross

Words by Fanny Crosby
Music by William H. Doane

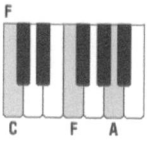

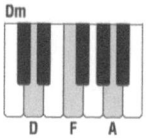

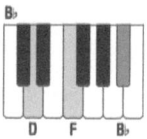

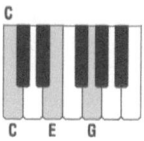

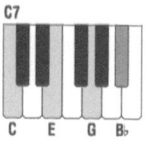

Verse 1

F **Dm** **B♭**
Jesus, keep me near the cross,

F **C**
There a precious fountain,

F **Dm** **B♭**
Free to all, a healing stream,

F **C7** **F**
Flows from Calv'ry's moun - tain.

Chorus 1

F **B♭**
In the cross, in the cross

F **B♭** **C**
Be my glory ever,

F **Dm** **B♭**
Till my raptured soul shall find

F **C7** **F**
Rest beyond the riv - er.

Copyright © 2015 by HAL LEONARD CORPORATION
International Copyright Secured All Rights Reserved

Verse 2

F **Dm** **B♭**
Near the cross, a trembling soul,

F **C**
Love and mercy found me.

F **Dm** **B♭**
There the Bright and Morning Star

F **C7** **F**
Sheds its beams a - round me.

Chorus 2

Repeat Chorus 1

Verse 3

F **Dm** **B♭**
Near the cross! Oh, Lamb of God,

F **C**
Bring its scenes be - fore me.

F **Dm** **B♭**
Help me walk from day to day

F **C7** **F**
With its shadow o'er me.

Chorus 3

Repeat Chorus 1

Verse 4

F **Dm** **B♭**
Near the cross! I'll watch and wait,

F **C**
Hoping, trusting ever,

F **Dm** **B♭**
Till I reach the golden strand,

F **C7** **F**
Just beyond the riv - er.

Chorus 4

Repeat Chorus 1

A New Name in Glory

Words and Music by
C. Austin Miles

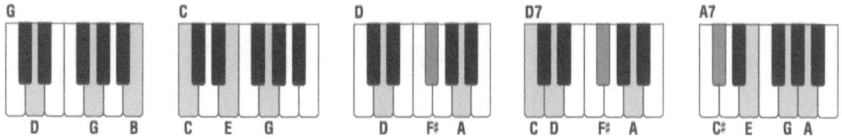

Verse 1

G C/G G G/B D G
I was once a sin - ner, but I came,

D7 G
Pardon to receive from my Lord.

C/G G G/B D G
This was freely giv - en, and I found

A7 D7
That He always kept His word.

Chorus 1

G
There's a new name written down in glory,

C G
And it's mine, O yes, it's mine.

D7 G
And the white robed angels sing the story,

A7 D7
"A sinner has come home."

G
For there's a new name written down in glory,

C G
And it's mine, O yes, it's mine.

C G C
With my sins forgiven I am bound for heav - en,

G D7 G
Never - more to roam.

Copyright © 2015 by HAL LEONARD CORPORATION
International Copyright Secured All Rights Reserved

Verse 2

G C/G G G/B D G
I was humbly kneel - ing at the cross,

D7 G
Fearing naught but God's angry frown,

C/G G G/B D G
When the heavens o - pened and I saw

A7 D7
That my name was written down.

Chorus 2

Repeat Chorus 1

Verse 3

G C/G G G/B D G
In the Book 'tis writ - ten, "Saved by grace."

D7 G
O the joy that came to my soul.

C/G G G/B D G
Now I am for - giv - en, and I know

A7 D7
By the blood I am made whole.

Chorus 3

Repeat Chorus 1

No, Not One!

Words by Johnson Oatman, Jr.
Music by George C. Hugg

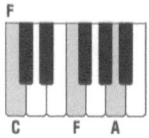

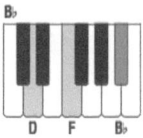

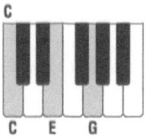

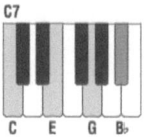

Verse 1

F **F/A** **B♭** **F**
There's not a friend like the lowly Je - sus,

C **F** **C7** **F**
No, not one! No, not one!

F/A **B♭** **F**
None else could heal all our soul's diseas - es,

C **F** **C7** **F**
No, not one! No, not one!

Chorus 1

F **C7** **F**
Jesus knows all about our strug - gles;

C
He will guide till the day is done.

F **F/A** **B♭** **F**
There's not a friend like the lowly Je - sus,

C **F** **C7** **F**
No, not one! No, not one!

Verse 2

F **F/A** **B♭** **F**
No friend like Him is so high and ho - ly,

C **F** **C7** **F**
No, not one! No, not one!

F/A **B♭** **F**
And yet no friend is so meek and low - ly,

C **F** **C7** **F**
No, not one! No, not one!

Chorus 2

Repeat Chorus 1

Copyright © 2015 by HAL LEONARD CORPORATION
International Copyright Secured All Rights Reserved

Verse 3

F F/A B♭ F
There's not an hour that He is not near us,

C F C7 F
No, not one! No, not one!

F/A B♭ F
No night so dark but His love can cheer us,

C F C7 F
No, not one! No, not one!

Chorus 3 *Repeat Chorus 1*

Verse 4

F F/A B♭ F
Did ever saint find this friend forsake him?

C F C7 F
No, not one! No, not one!

F/A B♭ F
Or sinner find that He would not take him?

C F C7 F
No, not one! No, not one!

Chorus 4 *Repeat Chorus 1*

Verse 5

F F/A B♭ F
Was e'er a gift like the Savior giv - en?

C F C7 F
No, not one! No, not one!

F/A B♭ F
Will He refuse us a home in heav - en?

C F C7 F
No, not one! No, not one!

Chorus 5 *Repeat Chorus 1*

Nothing But the Blood

Words and Music by
Robert Lowry

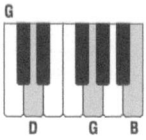

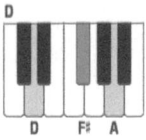

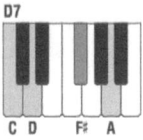

Verse 1

G D G
What can wash a - way my sin?

D7 G
Nothing but the blood of Je - sus.

D G
What can make me whole again?

D7 G
Nothing but the blood of Je - sus.

Chorus 1

G D G
Oh, pre - cious is the flow

D7 G/D D G
That makes me white as snow.

D G
No oth - er fount I know,

D7 G
Nothing but the blood of Je - sus.

Copyright © 2015 by HAL LEONARD CORPORATION
International Copyright Secured All Rights Reserved

Verse 2

G D G
For my par - don this I see,
D7 G
Nothing but the blood of Je - sus.
D G
For my cleans - ing, this my plea,
D7 G
Nothing but the blood of Je - sus.

Chorus 2

Repeat Chorus 1

Verse 3

G D G
Nothing can for sin atone,
D7 G
Nothing but the blood of Je - sus.
D G
Naught of good that I have done,
D7 G
Nothing but the blood of Je - sus.

Chorus 3

Repeat Chorus 1

Verse 4

G D G
This is all my hope and peace,
D7 G
Nothing but the blood of Je - sus.
D G
This is all my righteousness,
D7 G
Nothing but the blood of Je - sus.

Chorus 4

Repeat Chorus 1

Oh, How I Love Jesus

Words by Frederick Whitfield
Traditional American Melody

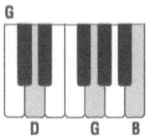

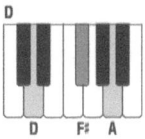

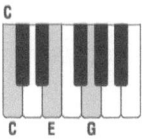

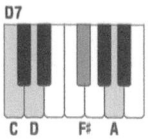

Verse 1

G D G
There is a name I love to hear, I love to sing its worth.

C G/D D7 G
It sounds like music in my ear, the sweetest name on earth.

Chorus 1

G D7 G
Oh, how I love Jesus! Oh, how I love Jesus!

C G/D D7 G
Oh, how I love Jesus, be - cause he first loved me.

Verse 2

G D G
It tells me of a Savior's love, who died to set me free.

C G/D D7 G
It tells me of His precious blood, the sinner's per - fect plea.

Chorus 2 *Repeat Chorus 1*

Verse 3

G D G
It tells me what my Father hath in store for ev'ry day,

C G/D D7 G
And though I tread a darksome path, yields sunshine all the way.

Chorus 3 *Repeat Chorus 1*

Verse 4

G D G
It tells of One whose loving heart can feel my deepest woe,

C G/D D7 G
Who in each sorrow bears a part, that none can bear be - low.

Chorus 4 *Repeat Chorus 1*

Copyright © 2015 by HAL LEONARD CORPORATION
International Copyright Secured All Rights Reserved

Revive Us Again

Words by William P. MacKay
Music by John J. Husband

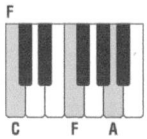

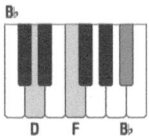

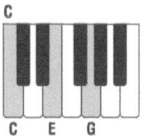

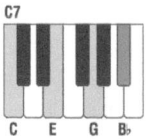

Verse 1

F
We praise Thee, O God, for the Son of Thy love,
B♭ F C
For Jesus, who died and is now gone above.

Chorus 1

F B♭ F
Halle - lu - jah! Thine the glory!
B♭ F C
Halle - lu - jah! A - men!
F B♭ F
Halle - lu - jah! Thine the glory!
B♭ F C7 F
Re - vive us a - gain.

Verse 2

F
We praise Thee, O God, for Thy Spirit of Light,
B♭ F C
Who has shown us our Sav - ior and scat - tered our night.

Chorus 2

Repeat Chorus 1

Verse 3

F
All glory and praise to the Lamb that was slain,
B♭ F C
Who has borne all our sins and has cleansed ev'ry stain.

Chorus 3

Repeat Chorus 1

Verse 4

F
Re - vive us again, fill each heart with Thy love.
B♭ F C
May each soul be re - kin - dled with fire from above.

Chorus 4

Repeat Chorus 1

Copyright © 2015 by HAL LEONARD CORPORATION
International Copyright Secured All Rights Reserved

The Old Rugged Cross

Words and Music by
Rev. George Bennard

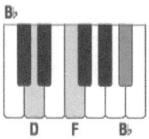

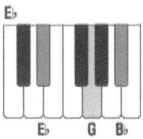

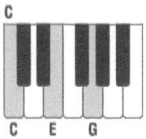

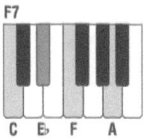

Verse 1

B♭ E♭
On a hill far away stood an old rugged cross,

C F7 B♭
The emblem of suff'ring and shame.

E♭
And I love that old cross, where the dearest and best

C F7 B♭
For a world of lost sinners was slain.

Chorus 1

F7 B♭
So I'll cherish the old rugged cross,

E♭ B♭
Till my trophies at last I lay down.

E♭
I will cling to the old rugged cross,

B♭ F7 B♭
And ex - change it some - day for a crown.

Copyright © 2015 by HAL LEONARD CORPORATION
International Copyright Secured All Rights Reserved

Verse 2

B♭ E♭
Oh, that old rugged cross, so de - spised by the world,

C F7 B♭
Has a wondrous attraction for me.

E♭
For the dear Lamb of God left His glory above

C F7 B♭
To bear it to dark Calva - ry.

Chorus 2 *Repeat Chorus 1*

Verse 3

B♭ E♭
In the old rugged cross, stained with blood so divine,

C F7 B♭
A wondrous beauty I see.

E♭
For 'twas on that old cross Jesus suffered and died

C F7 B♭
To pardon and sanctify me.

Chorus 3 *Repeat Chorus 1*

Verse 4

B♭ E♭
To the old rugged cross I will ever be true,

C F7 B♭
Its shame and reproach gladly bear.

E♭
Then He'll call me someday to my home far away,

C F7 B♭
Where His glory forever I'll share.

Chorus 4 *Repeat Chorus 1*

On Jordan's Stormy Banks

Words by Samuel Stennett
Traditional American Melody
Arranged by Rigdon M. McIntosh

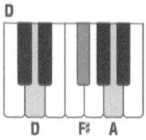

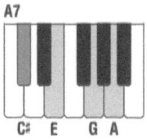

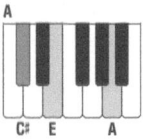

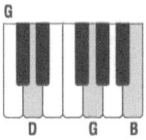

Verse 1

D **A7**
On Jordan's stormy banks I stand,

D **A**
And cast a wishful eye

A7 **D**
To Canaan's fair and happy land,

G **D** **A7** **D**
Where ___ my pos - sessions lie.

Chorus 1

D **A7**
I am bound for the Promised Land,

D **A**
I am bound for the Promised Land.

A7 **D**
O who will come and go with me?

G **D** **A7** **D**
I am bound for the Promised Land.

Copyright © 2015 by HAL LEONARD CORPORATION
International Copyright Secured All Rights Reserved

Verse 2

D **A7**
All o'er those wide ex - tended plains

D **A**
Shines one eternal day.

A7 **D**
There God the Son forever reigns,

G **D** **A7** **D**
And ___ scatters night a - way.

Chorus 2 *Repeat Chorus 1*

Verse 3

D **A7**
No chilling winds, nor pois'nous breath,

D **A**
Can reach that healthful shore.

A7 **D**
Sick - ness and sorrow, pain and death,

G **D** **A7** **D**
Are ___ felt and feared no more.

Chorus 3 *Repeat Chorus 1*

Verse 4

D **A7**
When shall I reach that happy place,

D **A**
And be forever blessed?

A7 **D**
When shall I see my Father's face,

G **D** **A7** **D**
And ___ in His bosom rest?

Chorus 4 *Repeat Chorus 1*

Pass Me Not, O Gentle Savior

Words by Fanny J. Crosby
Music by William H. Doane

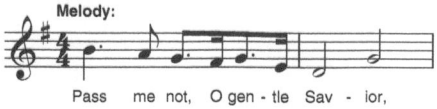

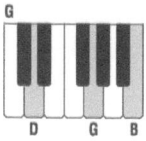

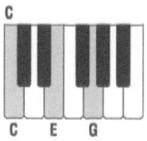

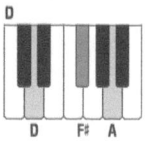

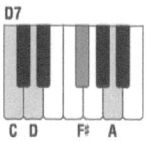

Verse 1

G G/B C G G/B
Pass me not, O gentle Sav - ior,

D G/B D G
Hear my hum - ble cry.

G/B C G G/B
While on others Thou art call - ing,

D7 G/D D7 G
Do not pass me by.

Chorus 1

G C G G/B D
Savior, Savior, hear my hum - ble cry.

G G/B C G G/B
While on others Thou art call - ing,

D7 G/D D7 G
Do not pass me by.

Copyright © 2015 by HAL LEONARD CORPORATION
International Copyright Secured All Rights Reserved

Verse 2

G G/B C G G/B
Let me at the throne of mer - cy

D G/B D G
Find a sweet re - lief.

G/B C G G/B
Kneel - ing there in deep con - tri - tion,

D7 G/D D7 G
Help my un - be - lief.

Chorus 2 *Repeat Chorus 1*

Verse 3

G G/B C G G/B
Trust - ing only in Thy mer - it,

D G/B D G
Would I seek Thy face.

G/B C G G/B
Heal my wounded, broken spir - it,

D7 G/D D7 G
Save me by Thy grace.

Chorus 3 *Repeat Chorus 1*

Verse 4

G G/B C G G/B
Thou, the Spring of all my com - fort,

D G/B D G
More than life to me,

G/B C G G/B
Whom have I on earth be - side Thee?

D7 G/D D7 G
Whom in heav'n but Thee?

Chorus 4 *Repeat Chorus 1*

Precious Memories

Words and Music by
J.B.F. Wright

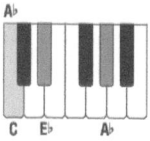

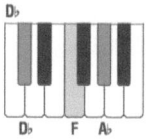

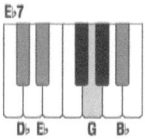

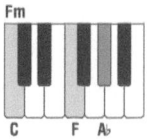

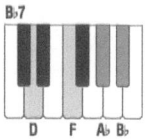

Verse 1

A♭ **D♭** **A♭**
Precious mem'ries, unseen an - gels,

E♭7 Fm **B♭7 E♭7**
Sent from somewhere to my soul.

A♭ **D♭** **A♭**
How they linger, ever near me,

A♭/C E♭7 Fm A♭ E♭7 A♭
And the sa - cred past un - fold.

Chorus 1

A♭
Precious mem'ries, how they linger,

D♭ **A♭**
How they ever flood my soul.

D♭ **A♭**
In the stillness of the mid - night,

A♭/C E♭7 Fm A♭ E♭7 A♭
Pre - cious sa - cred scenes un - fold.

Copyright © 2015 by HAL LEONARD CORPORATION
International Copyright Secured All Rights Reserved

Verse 2

A♭ D♭ A♭
Precious father, loving moth - er,

E♭7 Fm B♭7 E♭7
Fly a - cross the lonely years;

A♭ D♭ A♭
And old home scenes of my child - hood

A♭/C E♭7 Fm A♭ E♭7 A♭
In fond mem - o - ry ap - pear.

Chorus 2 *Repeat Chorus 1*

Verse 3

A♭ D♭ A♭
As I travel on life's path - way,

E♭7 Fm B♭7 E♭7
Know not what the years may hold.

A♭ D♭ A♭
As I ponder, hope grows fon - der,

A♭/C E♭7 Fm A♭ E♭7 A♭
Pre - cious mem - 'ries flood my soul.

Chorus 3 *Repeat Chorus 1*

Rock of Ages

Words by Augustus M. Toplady
V.1,2,4 altered by Thomas Cotterill
Music by Thomas Hastings

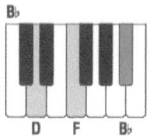

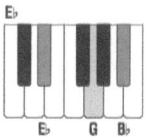

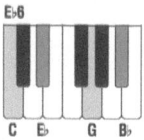

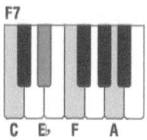

Verse 1

B♭ E♭ B♭
Rock of Ages, cleft for me,

B♭/D E♭6 B♭ F7 B♭
Let me hide myself in Thee.

F7 B♭
Let the water and the blood

F7 B♭
From Thy wounded side which flowed,

E♭ B♭ E♭ B♭
Be of sin the double cure,

B♭/D E♭6 B♭ F7 B♭
Save from wrath and make me pure.

Verse 2

B♭ E♭ B♭
Could my tears for - ever flow,

B♭/D E♭6 B♭ F7 B♭
Could my zeal no lan - guor know,

F7 B♭
These for sin could not a - tone,

F7 B♭
Thou must save, and Thou a - lone.

E♭ B♭ E♭ B♭
In my hand no price I bring,

B♭/D E♭6 B♭ F7 B♭
Sim - ply to Thy cross I cling.

Copyright © 2015 by HAL LEONARD CORPORATION
International Copyright Secured All Rights Reserved

Verse 3

B♭ E♭ B♭
Nothing in my hand I bring,

B♭/D E♭6 B♭ F7 B♭
Sim - ply to Thy cross I cling.

F7 B♭
Naked, come to Thee for dress,

F7 B♭
Helpless, look to Thee for grace.

E♭ B♭ E♭ B♭
Foul, I to the fountain fly,

B♭/D E♭6 B♭ F7 B♭
Wash me, Savior, or I die.

Verse 4

B♭ E♭ B♭
While I draw this fleeting breath,

B♭/D E♭6 B♭ F7 B♭
When my eyes shall close in death,

F7 B♭
When I rise to worlds un - known

F7 B♭
And be - hold Thee on Thy throne,

E♭ B♭ E♭ B♭
Rock of Ages, cleft for me,

B♭/D E♭6 B♭ F7 B♭
Let me hide myself in Thee.

Send the Light

Words and Music by
Charles H. Gabriel

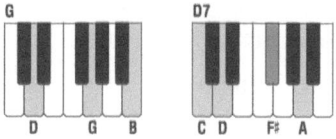

Verse 1

G
There's a call comes ringing o'er the restless wave,
D7 **G**
"Send the light! Send the light!"

There are souls to rescue, there are souls to save.
D7 **G**
Send the light! Send the light!

Chorus 1

G
Send the light, the blessed gospel light.
D7 **G**
Let it shine from shore to shore.

Send the light, the blessed gospel light,
D7 **G**
Let it shine forever - more.

Copyright © 2015 by HAL LEONARD CORPORATION
International Copyright Secured All Rights Reserved

Verse 2

G
We have heard the Macedonian call today,
D7 G
"Send the light! Send the light!"

And a golden off'ring at the cross we lay.
D7 G
Send the light! Send the light!

Chorus 2 *Repeat Chorus 1*

Verse 3

G
Let us pray that grace may ev'rywhere abound,
D7 G
"Send the light! Send the light!"

And a Christ-like Spirit ev'rywhere be found.
D7 G
Send the light! Send the light!

Chorus 3 *Repeat Chorus 1*

Verse 4

G
Let us not grow weary in the work of love,
D7 G
"Send the light! Send the light!"

Let us gather jewels for a crown above.
D7 G
Send the light! Send the light!

Chorus 4 *Repeat Chorus 1*

Shall We Gather at the River?

Words and Music by
Robert Lowry

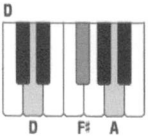

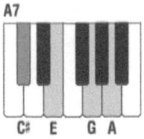

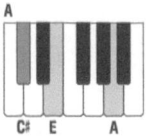

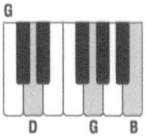

Verse 1

D **A7**
Shall we gather at the river, where bright angel feet have trod,
D **A** **A7** **D**
With its crystal tide forever flowing by the throne of God?

Chorus 1

G **D**
Yes, we'll gather at the river,
A7 **D**
The beautiful, the beautiful river.
G **D**
Gather with the saints at the river
A **A7** **D**
That flows by the throne of God.

Verse 2

D **A7**
On the bosom of the river, where the Savior King we own,
D **A** **A7** **D**
We shall meet, and sorrow never 'neath the glory of the throne.

Chorus 2 *Repeat Chorus 1*

Verse 3

D **A7**
Ere we reach the shining river, lay we ev'ry burden down.
D **A** **A7** **D**
Grace our spirits will deliver and pro - vide a robe and crown.

Chorus 3 *Repeat Chorus 1*

Verse 4

D **A7**
Soon we'll reach the shining river, soon our pilgrimage will cease.
D **A** **A7** **D**
Soon our happy hearts will quiver with the melo - dy of peace.

Chorus 4 *Repeat Chorus 1*

Copyright © 2015 by HAL LEONARD CORPORATION
International Copyright Secured All Rights Reserved

There Is a Balm in Gilead

African-American Spiritual

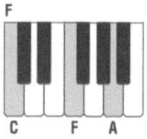

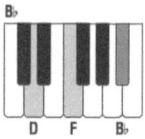

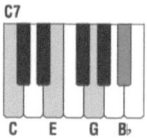

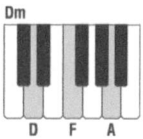

Chorus 1

F **B♭** **F C7**
There is a balm in Gilead to make the wound - ed whole.

F **C7** **F**
There is a balm in Gilead to heal the sin - sick soul.

Verse 1

F **B♭** **F** **C7**
Sometimes I feel dis - couraged, and think my works in vain,

F **B♭** **F** **C7** **Dm** **B♭**
But then the Holy Spirit re - vives my soul a - gain.

Chorus 2 *Repeat Chorus 1*

Verse 2

F **B♭** **F** **C7**
Don't ever feel dis - couraged, for Jesus is your friend.

F **B♭** **F** **C7** **Dm** **B♭**
And if you lack for knowledge, He'll not re - fuse to lend.

Chorus 3 *Repeat Chorus 1*

Verse 3

F **B♭** **F** **C7**
If you cannot preach like Peter, if you cannot pray like Paul,

F **B♭** **F** **C7** **Dm** **B♭**
You can tell the love of Jesus and say, "He died for all."

Chorus 4 *Repeat Chorus 1*

Copyright © 2015 by HAL LEONARD CORPORATION
International Copyright Secured All Rights Reserved

Since Jesus Came Into My Heart

Words by Rufus H. McDaniel
Music by Charles H. Gabriel

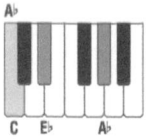

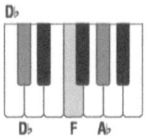

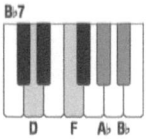

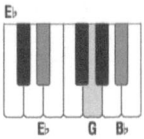

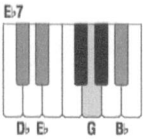

Verse 1

A♭
What a wonderful change in my life has been wrought
D♭ A♭
Since Jesus came into my heart.

I have light in my soul for which long I had sought,
B♭7 E♭ A♭ E♭7
Since Jesus came into my heart.

Chorus 1

A♭
Since Jesus came into my heart,
D♭ A♭
Since Jesus came into my heart;

Floods of joy o'er my soul like the sea billows roll,
D♭ A♭ E♭7 A♭
Since Jesus came into my heart.

Verse 2

A♭
I have ceased from my wand'ring and going astray,
D♭ A♭
Since Jesus came into my heart.

And my sins, which were many, are all washed away,
B♭7 E♭ A♭ E♭7
Since Jesus came into my heart.

Chorus 2

Repeat Chorus 1

Copyright © 2015 by HAL LEONARD CORPORATION
International Copyright Secured All Rights Reserved

Verse 3

A♭
I'm pos - sessed of a hope that is steadfast and sure,
D♭ A♭
Since Jesus came into my heart.

And no dark clouds of doubt now my pathway obscure,
B♭7 E♭ A♭ E♭7
Since Jesus came into my heart.

Chorus 3 *Repeat Chorus 1*

Verse 4

A♭
There's a light in the valley of death now for me,
D♭ A♭
Since Jesus came into my heart.

And the gates of the city beyond I can see,
B♭7 E♭ A♭ E♭7
Since Jesus came into my heart.

Chorus 4 *Repeat Chorus 1*

Verse 5

A♭
I shall go there to dwell in that city, I know,
D♭ A♭
Since Jesus came into my heart.

And I'm happy, so happy, as onward I go,
B♭7 E♭ A♭ E♭7
Since Jesus came into my heart.

Chorus 5 *Repeat Chorus 1*

Standing on the Promises

Words and Music by
R. Kelso Carter

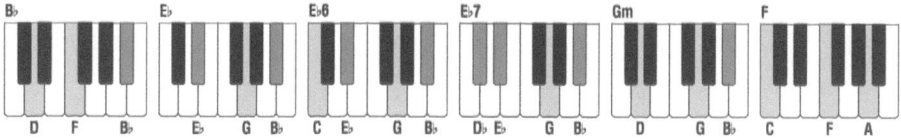

Verse 1

B♭
Standing on the promises of Christ my King!
E♭ **B♭**
Through eternal ages let His prais - es ring.

Glory in the highest I will shout and sing,
E♭6 **E♭7** **B♭**
Standing on the promis - es of God.

Chorus 1

B♭ **E♭** **Gm**
Standing, stand - ing,
F **B♭** **E♭** **B♭**
Standing on the promises of God my Sav - ior.
E♭
Standing, standing,
B♭ **E♭7** **B♭**
I'm standing on the promis - es of God.

Copyright © 2015 by HAL LEONARD CORPORATION
International Copyright Secured All Rights Reserved

Verse 2

B♭
Standing on the promises that cannot fail!
E♭ B♭
When the howling storms of doubt and fear assail,

By the living Word of God I shall prevail,
E♭6 E♭7 B♭
Standing on the promis - es of God.

Chorus 2 *Repeat Chorus 1*

Verse 3

B♭
Standing on the promises of Christ the Lord,
E♭ B♭
Bound to Him eternally by love's strong cord,

Overcoming daily with the Spirit's sword,
E♭6 E♭7 B♭
Standing on the promis - es of God.

Chorus 3 *Repeat Chorus 1*

Verse 4

B♭
Standing on the promises I cannot fall,
E♭ B♭
List'ning every moment to the Spir - it's call,

Resting in my Savior as my all and all,
E♭6 E♭7 B♭
Standing on the promis - es of God.

Chorus 4 *Repeat Chorus 1*

Sweet By and By

Words by Sanford Fillmore Bennett
Music by Joseph P. Webster

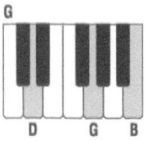

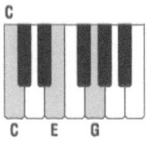

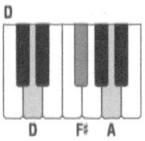

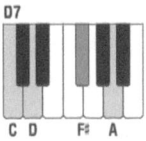

Verse 1

G **C** **G**
There's a land that is fairer than day,
D
And by faith we can see it a - far.
G **C** **G**
For the Father waits over the way
C **G/D** **D** **G**
To prepare us a dwell - ing place there.

Chorus 1

G **D**
In the sweet by and by,
D7 **G**
We shall meet on that beautiful shore.
G7/B **C**
In the sweet by and by,
G **D7** **G**
We shall meet on that beautiful shore.

Copyright © 2015 by HAL LEONARD CORPORATION
International Copyright Secured All Rights Reserved

Verse 2

G C G
We shall sing on that beautiful shore

D
The melodious songs of the blessed.

G C G
And our spirits shall sorrow no more,

C G/D D G
Not a sigh for the bless - ing of rest.

Chorus 2 *Repeat Chorus 1*

Verse 3

G C G
To our bountiful Father a - bove,

D
We will offer our tribute of praise

G C G
For the glorious gift of His love

C G/D D G
And the blessings that hal - low our days.

Chorus 3 *Repeat Chorus 1*

Sweet Hour of Prayer

Words by William W. Walford
Music by William B. Bradbury

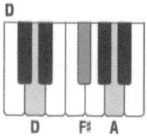

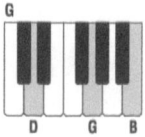

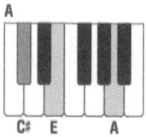

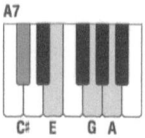

Verse 1

D G
Sweet hour of prayer, sweet hour of prayer,
D A D/A A
That calls me from a world of care,
D G
And bids me at my Father's throne
D A7 D
Make all my wants and wish - es known.
A7/E D/F♯ G D
In sea - sons of dis - tress and grief,
A7/E D/F♯ G D A
My soul has of - ten found re - lief,
D G
And oft escaped the tempter's snare
D A7 D
By thy return, sweet hour of prayer.

Verse 2

D G
Sweet hour of prayer, sweet hour of prayer,
D A D/A A
Thy joy I feel, the bliss I share
D G
Of those whose anxious spirits burn
D A7 D
With strong desire for thy re - turn.
A7/E D/F♯ G D
With such I has - ten to the place
A7/E D/F♯ G D A
Where God, my Sav - ior, shows His face,
D G
And gladly take my station there,
D A7 D
To wait for thee, sweet hour of prayer.

Copyright © 2015 by HAL LEONARD CORPORATION
International Copyright Secured All Rights Reserved

Verse 3

D G
Sweet hour of prayer, sweet hour of prayer,

D A D/A A
Thy wings shall my pe - ti - tion bear

D G
To Him, whose truth and faithfulness

D A7 D
En - gage the waiting soul to bless.

A7/E D/F♯ G D
And since He bids me seek His face,

A7/E D/F♯ G D A
Believe His Word, and trust His grace,

D G
I'll cast on Him my ev'ry care,

D A7 D
And wait for thee, sweet hour of prayer.

Verse 4

D G
Sweet hour of prayer, sweet hour of prayer,

D A D/A A
May I thy conso - la - tion share,

D G
Till from Mount Pisgah's lofty height

D A7 D
I view my home and take my flight.

A7/E D/F♯ G D
This robe of flesh I'll drop,

A7/E D/F♯ G D A
And rise to seize the ev - er - lasting prize,

D G
And shout, while passing through the air,

D A7 D
"Fare - well, farewell, sweet hour of prayer."

Tell It to Jesus

Words by Jeremiah E. Rankin
Music by Edmund S. Lorenz

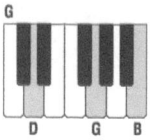

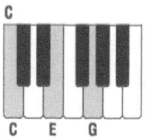

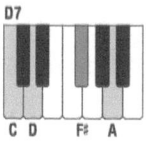

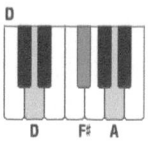

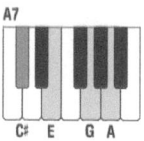

Verse 1

G G/B C G
Are you wea - ry, are you heavy hearted?

D7 G
Tell it to Jesus, tell it to Jesus.

G/B C G
Are you griev - ing over joys de - parted?

D7 G
Tell it to Jesus a - lone.

Chorus 1

D G G/B
Tell it to Jesus, tell it to Je - sus,

C G D A7 D D7
He is a friend that's well - known.

G G/B C G
You've no oth - er such a friend or brother,

D7 G
Tell it to Jesus a - lone.

Copyright © 2015 by HAL LEONARD CORPORATION
International Copyright Secured All Rights Reserved

Verse 2

G G/B C G
Do the tears flow down your cheeks un - bidden?

D7 G
Tell it to Jesus, tell it to Jesus.

G/B C G
Have you sins that to men's eyes are hidden?

D7 G
Tell it to Jesus a - lone.

Chorus 2

Repeat Chorus 1

Verse 3

G G/B C G
Do you fear the gath'ring clouds of sorrow?

D7 G
Tell it to Jesus, tell it to Jesus.

G/B C G
Are you anx - ious what shall be to - morrow?

D7 G
Tell it to Jesus a - lone.

Chorus 3

Repeat Chorus 1

Verse 4

G G/B C G
Are you trou - bled at the thought of dying?

D7 G
Tell it to Jesus, tell it to Jesus.

G/B C G
For Christ's com - ing kingdom are you sighing?

D7 G
Tell it to Jesus a - lone.

Chorus 4

Repeat Chorus 1

There Is a Fountain

Words by William Cowper
Traditional American Melody
Arranged by Lowell Mason

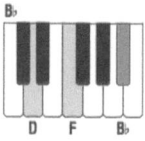

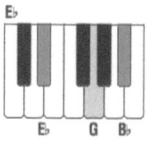

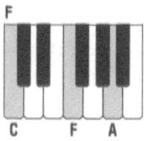

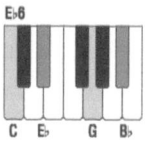

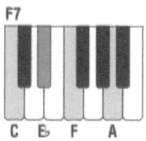

Verse 1

B♭ B♭/D E♭ B♭
There is a foun - tain filled with blood

F
Drawn from Immanuel's veins;

B♭ B♭/D E♭ B♭
And sinners, plunged be - neath that flood,

B♭/D E♭6 B♭ F7 B♭
Lose _____ all their guilty stains:

F B♭ E♭
Lose all their guilt - y stains,

B♭ F
Lose all their guilty stains.

B♭ B♭/D E♭ B♭
And sinners, plunged be - neath that flood,

B♭/D E♭6 B♭ F7 B♭
Lose _____ all their guilty stains.

Copyright © 2015 by HAL LEONARD CORPORATION
International Copyright Secured All Rights Reserved

Verse 2

B♭ B♭/D E♭ B♭
The dying thief re - joiced to see

F
That fountain in his day;

B♭ B♭/D E♭ B♭
And there may I, though vile as he,

B♭/D E♭6 B♭ F7 B♭
Wash _____ all my sins a - way;

F B♭ E♭
Wash all my sins a - way,

B♭ F
Wash all my sins a - way.

B♭ B♭/D E♭ B♭
And there may I, though vile as he,

B♭/D E♭6 B♭ F7 B♭
Wash _____ all my sins a - way.

Verse 3

B♭ B♭/D E♭ B♭
Dear dying Lamb, Thy precious blood

F
Shall never lose its pow'r,

B♭ B♭/D E♭ B♭
Till all the ran - somed Church of God

B♭/D E♭6 B♭ F7 B♭
Be _____ saved to sin no more:

F B♭ E♭
Be saved, to sin no more,

B♭ F
Be saved to sin no more.

B♭ B♭/D E♭ B♭
Till all the ran - somed Church of God

B♭/D E♭6 B♭ F7 B♭
Be _____ saved, to sin no more.

Verse 4

B♭ B♭/D E♭ B♭
E'er since, by faith, I saw the stream

F
Thy flowing wounds sup - ply,

B♭ B♭/D E♭ B♭
Re - deeming love has been my theme,

B♭/D E♭6 B♭ F7 B♭
And _____ shall be till I die:

F B♭ E♭
And shall be till I die,

B♭ F
And shall be till I die.

B♭ B♭/D E♭ B♭
Re - deeming love has been my theme,

B♭/D E♭6 B♭ F7 B♭
And _____ shall be till I die.

Verse 5

B♭ B♭/D E♭ B♭
When this poor lisp - ing, stamm'ring tongue

F
Lies silent in the grave,

B♭ B♭/D E♭ B♭
Then in a no - bler, sweeter song

B♭/D E♭6 B♭ F7 B♭
I'll _____ sing Thy pow'r to save:

F B♭ E♭
I'll sing Thy pow'r to save,

B♭ F
I'll sing Thy pow'r to save.

B♭ B♭/D E♭ B♭
Then in a no - bler, sweeter song

B♭/D E♭6 B♭ F7 B♭
I'll _____ sing Thy pow'r to save.

When I Can Read My Title Clear

Words by Isaac Watts
Traditional American Melody
Attributed to Joseph C. Lowry

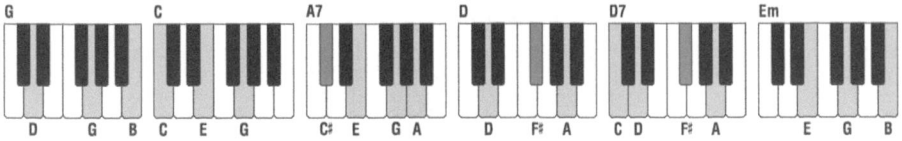

Verse 1

G C G
When I can read my title clear
C G/B A7 D
To mansions in the skies,
G D7
I'll bid farewell to ev'ry fear
Em C G/D C/D D7 G
And wipe my weep - ing ____ eyes,
C G
And wipe my weeping eyes,
C G/B A7 D
And wipe my weep - ing eyes.
G D7
I'll bid farewell to ev'ry fear
Em C G/D C/D D7 G
And wipe my weep - ing ____ eyes.

Copyright © 2015 by HAL LEONARD CORPORATION
International Copyright Secured All Rights Reserved

Verse 2

G C G
Should earth against my soul en - gage,

C G/B A7 D
And hellish darts be hurled,

G D7
Then I can smile at Satan's rage

Em C G/D C/D D7 G
And face a frown - ing ____ world,

C G
And face a frowning world,

C G/B A7 D
And face a frown - ing world.

G D7
Then I can smile at Satan's rage

Em C G/D C/D D7 G
And face a frown - ing ____ world.

Verse 3

G C G
Let cares like a wild deluge come,

C G/B A7 D
And storms of sor - row fall,

G D7
May I but safely reach my home,

Em C G/D C/D D7 G
My God, my heav'n, my ____ all.

C G
My God, my heav'n, my all,

C G/B A7 D
My God, my heav'n, my all,

G D7
May I but safely reach my home,

Em C G/D C/D D7 G
My God, my heav'n, my ____ all.

Verse 4

G **C** **G**
There shall I bathe my weary soul

C **G/B** **A7** **D**
In seas of heav'n - ly rest,

G **D7**
And not a wave of trouble roll

Em **C** **G/D** **C/D** **D7** **G**
A - cross my peace - ful ____ breast,

C **G**
Across my peaceful breast,

C **G/B** **A7** **D**
Across my peace - ful breast.

G **D7**
And not a wave of trouble roll

Em **C** **G/D** **C/D** **D7** **G**
A - cross my peace - ful ____ breast.

There Is Power in the Blood

Words and Music by
Lewis E. Jones

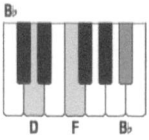

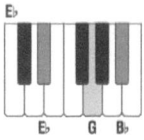

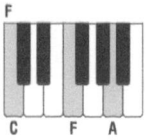

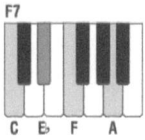

Verse 1

B♭ **E♭** **B♭**
Would you be free from your burden of sin?

F **B♭**
There's pow'r in the blood, pow'r in the blood.

E♭ **B♭**
Would you o'er evil a victory win?

F7 **B♭**
There's wonderful pow'r in the blood.

Chorus 1

B♭ **E♭** **B♭**
There is pow'r, pow'r, wonderworking pow'r

F7 **B♭**
In the blood of the Lamb.

E♭ **B♭**
There is pow'r, pow'r, wonderworking pow'r

F7 **B♭** **F7** **B♭**
In the precious blood of the Lamb.

Copyright © 2015 by HAL LEONARD CORPORATION
International Copyright Secured All Rights Reserved

Verse 2

B♭ E♭ B♭
Would you be free from your passion and pride?

F B♭
There's pow'r in the blood, pow'r in the blood.

E♭ B♭
Come for a cleansing to Calvary's tide.

F7 B♭
There's wonderful pow'r in the blood.

Chorus 2

Repeat Chorus 1

Verse 3

B♭ E♭ B♭
Would you be whiter, much whiter than snow?

F B♭
There's pow'r in the blood, pow'r in the blood.

E♭ B♭
Sin-stains are lost in its life-giving flow.

F7 B♭
There's wonderful pow'r in the blood.

Chorus 3

Repeat Chorus 1

Verse 4

B♭ E♭ B♭
Would you do service for Jesus, your King?

F B♭
There's pow'r in the blood, pow'r in the blood.

E♭ B♭
Would you live daily His praises to sing?

F7 B♭
There's wonderful pow'r in the blood.

Chorus 4

Repeat Chorus 1

'Tis So Sweet to Trust in Jesus

Words by Louisa M.R. Stead
Music by William J. Kirkpatrick

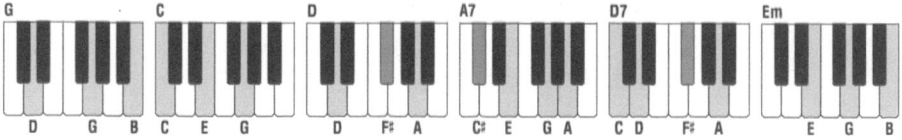

Verse 1

G C G
'Tis so sweet to trust in Je - sus,
D/F♯ A7/E D
Just to take Him at His Word.
G C G
Just to rest up - on His prom - ise,
C G D G
Just to know, "Thus saith the Lord."

Chorus 1

G D7 Em G D
Jesus, Jesus, how I trust Him,
G D/F♯ A7/E D
How I've proved Him o'er and o'er.
G G/B C G
Jesus, Je - sus, precious Je - sus!
C G D G
O for grace to trust Him more!

Copyright © 2015 by HAL LEONARD CORPORATION
International Copyright Secured All Rights Reserved

Verse 2

G C G
O how sweet to trust in Je - sus,
D/F♯ A7/E D
Just to trust His cleans - ing blood.
G C G
Just in simple faith to plunge me
C G D G
'Neath the healing, cleans - ing flood.

Chorus 2

Repeat Chorus 1

Verse 3

G C G
Yes, 'tis sweet to trust in Je - sus,
D/F♯ A7/E D
Just from sin and self to cease.
G C G
Just from Jesus simply tak - ing
C G D G
Life and rest, and joy and peace.

Chorus 3

Repeat Chorus 1

Verse 4

G C G
I'm so glad I learned to trust Thee,
D/F♯ A7/E D
Precious Jesus, Sav - ior, Friend.
G C G
And I know that Thou art with me,
C G D G
Wilt be with me to the end.

Chorus 4

Repeat Chorus 1

Turn Your Eyes Upon Jesus

Words and Music by
Helen H. Lemmel

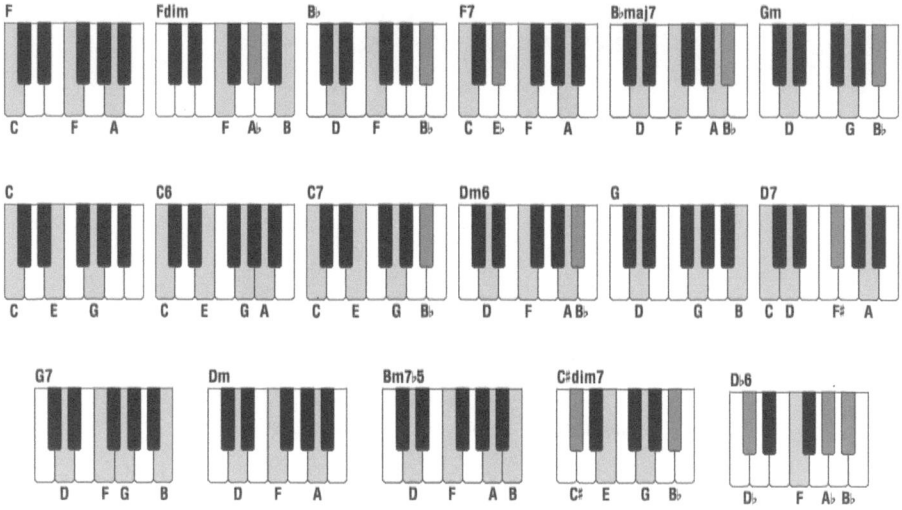

Verse 1

F Fdim F B♭/D F7/C B♭maj7 Gm
O soul, are you wea - ry and troub - led?

F/C C F/C C6 C7 F
No light in the dark - ness you see?

Fdim F B♭ F Dm6/F C/E
There's light for a look at the Sav - ior,

C F G/F D7/F♯ C G7 C
And life more a - bun - dant and free.

Chorus 1

F C C7 Dm F7/C
Turn your eyes up - on Je - sus.

B♭ Bm7♭5 C
Look full in His wonder - ful face,

F C♯dim7 Dm F7/C B♭
And the things of earth will grow strange - ly dim

Dm D♭6 F/C C F/C C7 F
In the light of His glory and grace.

Copyright © 2015 by HAL LEONARD CORPORATION
International Copyright Secured All Rights Reserved

Verse 2

F Fdim F B♭/D F7/C B♭maj7 Gm
Through death in - to life ev - er - last - ing

F/C C F/C C6 C7 F
He passed, and we fol - low Him there.

Fdim F B♭ F Dm6/F C/E
Over us sin no more hath do - min - ion,

C F G/F D7/F♯ C G7 C
For more ___ than con - qu'rors we are.

Chorus 2 *Repeat Chorus 1*

Verse 3

F Fdim F B♭/D F7/C B♭maj7 Gm
His word shall not fail you, He prom - ised.

F/C C F/C C6 C7 F
Be - lieve Him, and all will be well:

Fdim F B♭ F Dm6/F C/E
Then go to a world that is dy - ing,

C F G/F D7/F♯ C G7 C
His per - fect sal - va - tion to tell.

Chorus 3 *Repeat Chorus 1*

The Unclouded Day

Words and Music by
J.K. Alwood

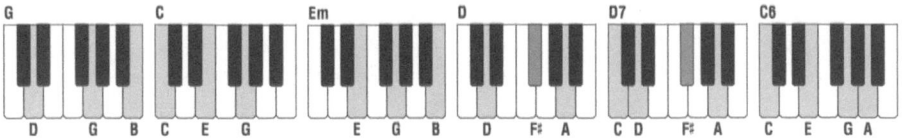

Verse 1

G C G
O they tell me of a home far be - yond the skies,

Em D
O they tell me of a home far a - way.

D7 G C G
O they tell me of a home were no storm clouds rise,

G/B C6 G/D D7 G
O they tell me of an un - clouded day.

Chorus 1

G
O the land of cloudless day,

D
O the land of an unclouded sky,

D7 G C G
O they tell me of a home were no storm clouds rise,

G/B C6 G/D D7 G
O they tell me of an un - clouded day.

Copyright © 2015 by HAL LEONARD CORPORATION
International Copyright Secured All Rights Reserved

Verse 2

G **C** **G**
O they tell me of a home where my friends have gone,

Em **D**
O they tell me of that land far a - way,

D7 **G** **C** **G**
Where the tree of life in e - ternal bloom

G/B **C6** **G/D** **D7** **G**
Sheds its fragrance through the un - clouded day.

Chorus 2 *Repeat Chorus 1*

Verse 3

G **C** **G**
O they tell me of a King in His beauty there,

Em **D**
And they tell me that mine eyes shall be - hold

D7 **G** **C** **G**
Where He sits on the throne that is whiter than snow,

G/B **C6** **G/D** **D7** **G**
In the city that is made of gold.

Chorus 3 *Repeat Chorus 1*

Verse 4

G **C** **G**
O they tell me that He smiles on His children there,

Em **D**
And His smile drives their sorrows all a - way.

D7 **G** **C** **G**
And they tell me that no tears ever come a - gain

G/B **C6** **G/D** **D7** **G**
In that lovely land of un - clouded day.

Chorus 4 *Repeat Chorus 1*

Wayfaring Stranger

Southern American Folk Hymn

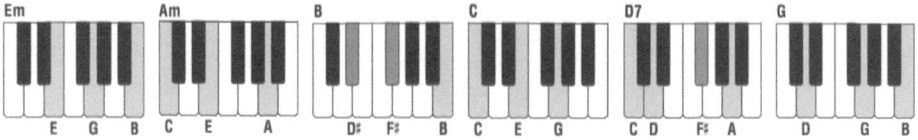

Verse 1

Em
I am a poor wayfaring stranger

Am **B**
While trav'ling through this world of woe,

Yet there's no sickness, toil, nor danger

Am **Em**
In that bright world to which I go.

C **D7** **G**
I'm going there to see my Father,

C **D7** **Em**
I'm going there no more to roam;

I'm only going over Jordan,

Am **Em**
I'm only going over home.

Copyright © 2010 by HAL LEONARD CORPORATION
International Copyright Secured All Rights Reserved

Verse 2

Em
I know dark clouds will gather 'round me,
Am **B**
I know my way is rough and steep;

But golden fields lie out before me
Am **Em**
Where God's re-deemed shall ever sleep.
C **D7** **G**
I'm going there to see my mother,
C **D7** **Em**
She said she'd meet me when I come;

I'm only going over Jordan,
Am **Em**
I'm only going over home.

Verse 3

Em
I'll soon be free from ev'ry trial,
Am **B**
My body sleep in the church-yard;

I'll drop the cross of self-denial
Am **Em**
And enter on my greatest re-ward.
C **D7** **G**
I'm going there to see my Savior,
C **D7** **Em**
To sing His praise for-ever-more;

I'm only going over Jordan,
Am **Em**
I'm only going over home.

We'll Understand It Better By and By

Words and Music by
Charles A. Tindley

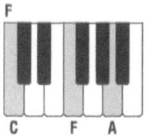

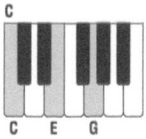

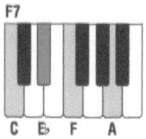

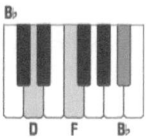

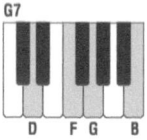

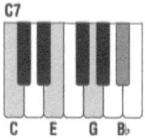

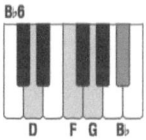

Verse 1

F C F7 B♭ F
Trials dark on ev'ry hand, and we cannot under - stand

C G7 C7
All the ways that God would lead us to that blessed Promised Land.

F C F7 B♭ F
But He'll guide us with His eye, and we'll follow till we die.

B♭6 F C7 F
We will understand it better by and by.

Chorus 1

F F7 B♭ F
By and by, ___ when the morning comes,

C G7 C7
When the Saints of God are gathered home,

F F7 B♭ F
We will tell the sto - ry how we've over - come,

G7 F C7 F
We will understand it better by and by.

Copyright © 2015 by HAL LEONARD CORPORATION
International Copyright Secured All Rights Reserved

Verse 2

F C F7 B♭ F
Oft our cherished plans have failed, dis - ap - pointments have pre - vailed,

C G7 C7
And we've wandered in the darkness, heavy hearted and a - lone.

F C F7 B♭ F
But we're trusting in the Lord and, ac - cording to His Word,

B♭6 F C7 F
We will understand it better by and by.

Chorus 2 *Repeat Chorus 1*

Verse 3

F C F7 B♭ F
Temp - tations, hidden snares of - ten take us un - awares,

C G7 C
And our hearts are made to bleed for some thoughtless word or deed.

F C F7 B♭ F
And we wonder why the test when we try to do our best,

B♭6 F C7 F
But we'll understand it better by and by.

Chorus 3 *Repeat Chorus 1*

What a Friend We Have in Jesus

Words by Joseph M. Scriven
Music by Charles C. Converse

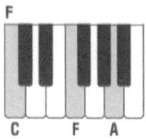

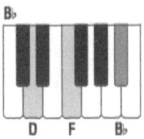

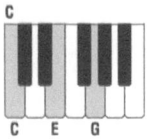

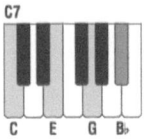

Verse 1

F B♭ F B♭
What a Friend we have in Jesus,

F C
All our sins and grief to bear.

F B♭ F B♭
What a priv - ilege to carry

F C7 F
Ev'rything to God in prayer!

C F
O what peace we often forfeit,

B♭ F C7 F C
O what needless pain we bear,

F B♭ F B♭
All be - cause we do not carry

F C7 F
Ev'rything to God in prayer!

Copyright © 2015 by HAL LEONARD CORPORATION
International Copyright Secured All Rights Reserved

Verse 2

F B♭ F B♭
Have we tri - als and temp - tations?

F C
Is there trouble any - where?

F B♭ F B♭
We should nev - er be dis - couraged,

F C7 F
Take it to the Lord in prayer.

C F
Can we find a friend so faithful

B♭ F C7 F C
Who will all our sor - rows share?

F B♭ F B♭
Jesus knows our ev'ry weakness,

F C7 F
Take it to the Lord in prayer.

Verse 3

F B♭ F B♭
Are we weak and heavy laden,

F C
Cumbered with a load of care?

F B♭ F B♭
Precious Sav - ior, still our refuge,

F C7 F
Take it to the Lord in prayer.

C F
Do thy friends despise, for - sake thee?

B♭ F C7 F C
Take it to the Lord in prayer.

F B♭ F B♭
In His arms He'll take and shield thee,

F C7 F
Thou wilt find a sol - ace there.

When the Roll Is Called Up Yonder

Words and Music by
James M. Black

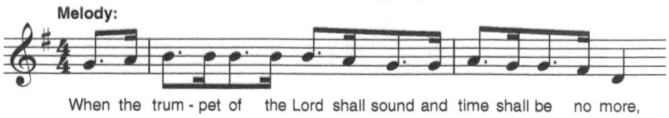

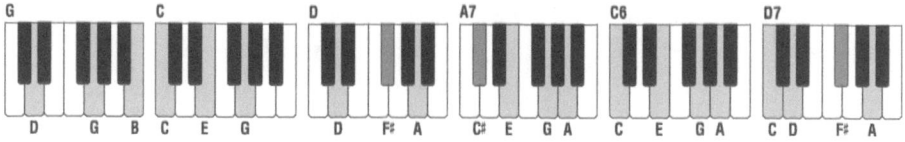

Verse 1

G G/B C G
When the trumpet of the Lord shall sound, and time shall be no more,

D/F♯ A7/E D
And the morning breaks, eternal, bright and fair,

G G/B C G
When the saved of earth shall gather over on the other shore,

G/B C6 G D7 G
And the roll is called up yonder, I'll be there.

Chorus 1

G
When the roll is called up yonder,

D7
When the roll is called up yonder,

G C
When the roll is called up yonder,

G D7 G
When the roll is called up yonder, I'll be there.

Copyright © 2015 by HAL LEONARD CORPORATION
International Copyright Secured All Rights Reserved

Verse 2

G G/B C G
On that bright and cloudless morning when the dead in Christ shall rise,

D/F♯ A7/E D
And the glory of His resur - rec - tion share;

G G/B C G
When His chosen ones shall gather to their home beyond the skies,

G/B C6 G D7 G
And the roll is called up yonder, I'll be there.

Chorus 2 *Repeat Chorus 1*

Verse 3

G G/B C G
Let us labor for the Master from the dawn till setting sun,

D/F♯ A7/E D
Let us talk of all His wondrous love and care.

G G/B C G
Then when all of life is over, and our work on earth is done,

G/B C6 G D7 G
And the roll is called up yonder, I'll be there.

Chorus 3 *Repeat Chorus 1*

When the Saints Go Marching In

Words by Katherine E. Purvis
Music by James M. Black

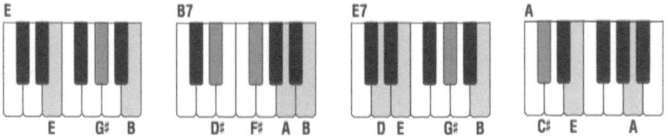

Verse 1

E
Oh, when the saints go marching in,
B7
Oh, when the saints go marching in,
E E7 A
Oh Lord, I want to be in that number,
E B7 E
When the saints go marching in.

Verse 2

E
Oh, when the sun refuse to shine,
B7
Oh, when the sun refuse to shine,
E E7 A
Oh Lord, I want to be in that number,
E B7 E
When the sun re-fuse to shine.

Copyright © 2010 by HAL LEONARD CORPORATION
International Copyright Secured All Rights Reserved

Verse 3

E
Oh, when they crown Him Lord of all,

B7
Oh, when they crown Him Lord of all,

E E7 A
Oh Lord, I want to be in that number,

E B7 E
When they crown Him Lord of all.

Verse 4

E
Oh, when they gather 'round the throne,

B7
Oh, when they gather 'round the throne,

E E7 A
Oh Lord, I want to be in that number,

E B7 E
When they gather 'round the throne.

When We All Get to Heaven

Words by Eliza E. Hewitt
Music by Emily D. Wilson

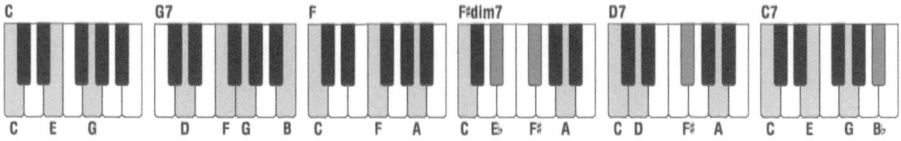

Verse 1

C
Sing the wond'rous love of Jesus,
G7 C
Sing His mercy and His grace.
F F♯°7
In the mansions bright and bless - ed,
C/G G7 C
He'll pre - pare for us a place.

Chorus 1

C
When we all get to heaven,
D7 G7
What a day of re - joicing that will be!
C C7 F
When we all see Jesus,
F♯°7 C/G G7 C F C
We'll sing and shout the victo - ry.

Copyright © 2015 by HAL LEONARD CORPORATION
International Copyright Secured All Rights Reserved

Verse 2

C
While we walk the pilgrim pathway,
G7 **C**
Clouds will overspread the sky.
F **F♯°7**
But when trav'ling days are o - ver,
C/G G7 **C**
Not a shadow, not a sigh.

Chorus 2

Repeat Chorus 1

Verse 3

C
Let us then be true and faithful,
G7 **C**
Trusting, serving ev'ry day.
F **F♯°7**
Just one glimpse of Him in glo - ry
C/G G7 **C**
Will the toils of life re - pay.

Chorus 3

Repeat Chorus 1

Verse 4

C
Onward to the prize before us!
G7 **C**
Soon His beauty we'll be - hold;
F **F♯°7**
Soon the pearly gates will o - pen;
C/G G7 **C**
We shall tread the streets of gold.

Chorus 4

Repeat Chorus 1

Whispering Hope

Words and Music by
Alice Hawthorne

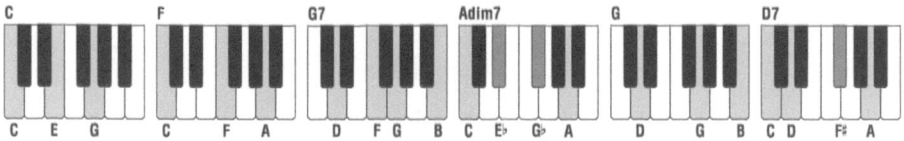

Verse 1

C F C
Soft as the voice of an angel,

G7 C
Breathing a lesson un - heard,

F
Hope with a gentle per - suasion

C G7 C
Whispers her comforting word:

Adim7 G7/B C
Wait till the dark - ness is over,

G D7 G G7
Wait till the tempest is done.

C F C
Hope for the sunshine to - morrow,

G7 C
After the shower is gone.

Chorus 1

G7 C G7 C
Whispering hope, O how welcome Thy voice,

F C G7 C
Making my heart in its sorrow re - joice.

Copyright © 2015 by HAL LEONARD CORPORATION
International Copyright Secured All Rights Reserved

Verse 2

C F C
If, in the dusk of the twilight,
G7 C
Dim be the region a - far,
F
Will not the deepening darkness
C G7 C
Brighten the glimmering star?
Adim7 G7/B C
Then when the night is up - on us,
G D7 G G7
Why should the heart sink a - way?
C F C
When the dark midnight is over,
G7 C
Watch for the breaking of day.

Chorus 2

Repeat Chorus 1

Verse 3

C F C
Hope, as an anchor so steadfast,
G7 C
Rends the dark veil for the soul,
F
Whither the Master has entered,
C G7 C
Robbing the grave of its goal.
Adim7 G7/B C
Come then, O come, glad fru - ition,
G D7 G G7
Come to my sad weary heart.
C F C
Come, O Thou blest hope of glory,
G7 C
Never, O never de - part.

Chorus 3

Repeat Chorus 1

Whiter Than Snow

Words by James L. Nicholson
Music by William G. Fischer

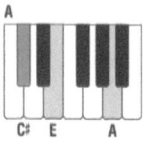

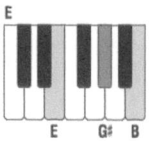

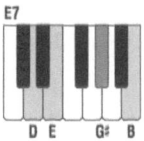

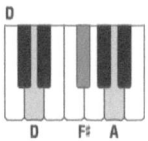

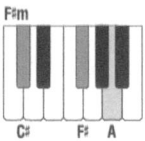

Verse 1

A E A E7 A
Lord Jesus, I long to be perfectly whole;

E A E7 A
I want Thee for - ever to live in my soul;

A/C♯ D A
Break down ev - 'ry idol, cast out ev'ry foe;

E7 A
Now wash me and I shall be whiter than snow.

Chorus 1

E7 F♯m D A
Whiter than snow, yes, whiter than snow;

D A E7 A
Now wash me, and I shall be whiter than snow.

Copyright © 2015 by HAL LEONARD CORPORATION
International Copyright Secured All Rights Reserved

Verse 2

A E A E7 A
Lord Jesus, look down from Thy throne in the skies,
E A E7 A
And help me to make a com - plete sacri - fice;
A/C♯ D A
I give up my - self and whatever I know,
E7 A
Now wash me, and I shall be whiter than snow.

Chorus 2 *Repeat Chorus 1*

Verse 3

A E A E7 A
Lord Jesus, for this I most humbly en - treat,
E A E7 A
I wait, bless - ed Lord, at Thy crucified feet;
A/C♯ D A
By faith, for my cleansing, I see Thy blood flow,
E7 A
Now wash me, and I shall be whiter than snow.

Chorus 3 *Repeat Chorus 1*

Verse 4

A E A E7 A
Lord Jesus, be - fore You I patiently wait;
E A E7 A
Come now and with - in me a new heart cre - ate;
A/C♯ D A
To those who have sought Thee, Thou never saidst, "No."
E7 A
Now wash me, and I shall be whiter than snow.

Chorus 4 *Repeat Chorus 1*

Will the Circle Be Unbroken

Words by Ada R. Habershon
Music by Charles H. Gabriel

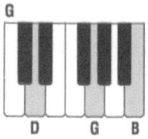

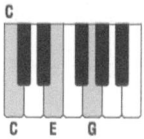

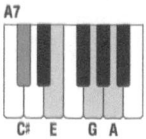

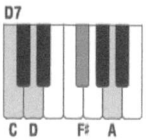

Verse 1

G C G
I was standing by my window on one cold and cloudy day,

A7 D7
When I saw the hearse come rolling, for to take my mother a - way.

Chorus 1

G C G
Will the circle be unbroken, by and by, Lord, by and by?

C G D7 G
There's a better home a - waiting in the sky, in the sky.

Verse 2

G C G
Oh, I told the undertaker, "Under - taker, please drive slow,

A7 D7
For this body you are hauling, Lord, I hate to see her go."

Chorus 2 *Repeat Chorus 1*

Verse 3

G C G
I will follow close behind her, try to hold up and be brave,

A7 D7
But I could not hide my sorrow when they laid her in the grave.

Chorus 3 *Repeat Chorus 1*

Copyright © 2015 by HAL LEONARD CORPORATION
International Copyright Secured All Rights Reserved

Wonderful Grace of Jesus

Words and Music by
Haldor Lillenas

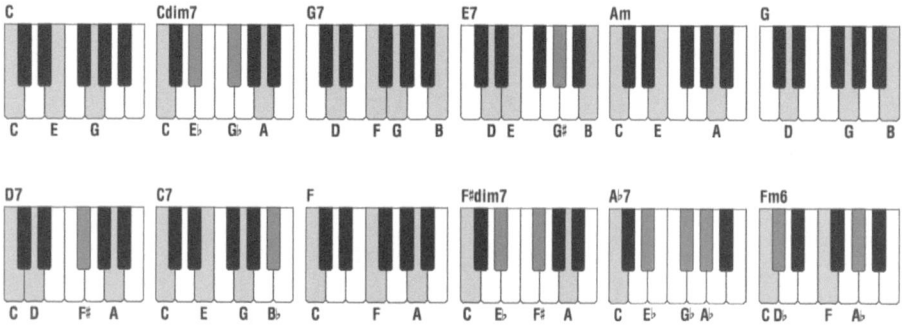

Verse 1

C **Cdim7 C**
Wonderful grace of Je - sus,

G7 **C E7**
Greater than all my sin.

Am
How shall my tongue describe it,

G **D7** **G G7**
Where shall its praise be - gin?

C **Cdim7 C**
Taking away my bur - den,

C7 **F**
Setting my spirit free,

Copyright © 2015 by HAL LEONARD CORPORATION
International Copyright Secured All Rights Reserved

Chorus 1

F♯dim7 D7 C A♭7
For the wonderful grace of Je - sus

C G7 C
Reach - es me.

G7
Wonderful, the matchless grace of Jesus,

C G7
Deeper than the mighty rolling sea.

C
Higher than the mountain, sparkling like a fountain,

D7 G
All sufficient grace for even me.

C G
Broader than the scope of my trans - gressions,

C C7 F
Greater far than all my sin and shame.

F♯dim7 C C/B♭ F/A Fm6/A♭
O magnify the precious name of Je - sus,

C G7 C
Praise His name!

Verse 2

C **Cdim7 C**
Wonderful grace of Je - sus,

G7 **C** **E7**
Reaching to all the lost.

Am
By it I have been pardoned,

G **D7** **G** **G7**
Saved to the utter - most.

C **Cdim7 C**
Chains have been torn a - sun - der,

C7 **F**
Giving me liber - ty.

Chorus 2

Repeat Chorus 1

Verse 3

C **Cdim7 C**
Wonderful grace of Je - sus,

G7 **C** **E7**
Reaching the most de - filed,

Am
By its transforming power,

G **D7** **G** **G7**
Making him God's dear child,

C **Cdim7 C**
Purchasing peace and heav - en

C7 **F**
For all e - terni - ty.

Chorus 3

Repeat Chorus 1

Wonderful Peace

Words by W.D. Cornell
Music by W.G. Cooper

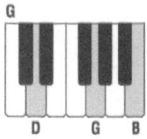

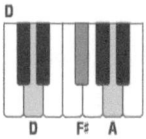

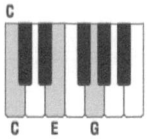

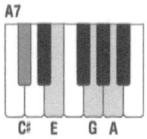

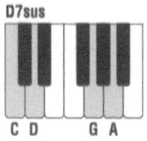

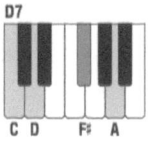

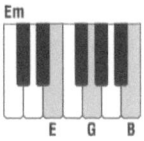

Verse 1

G **D/A** **G/B** **C** **G**
Far a - way in the depths of my spirit to - night

A7 **D7sus** **D7**
Rolls a melody sweeter than psalm.

G **D/A** **G/B** **C**
In ce - lestial-like strains it un - ceasingly falls

G **D7** **G**
O'er my soul like an in - finite calm.

Chorus 1

G **G/B** **C** **G**
Peace! Peace! Wonderful peace,

Em **A7** **D**
Coming down from the Father a - bove.

G **D/A** **G/B** **C**
Sweep over my spir - it for - ever, I pray,

G **D7** **G**
In fathomless billows of love.

Verse 2

G **D/A** **G/B** **C** **G**
What a treasure I have in this wonderful peace,

A7 **D7sus** **D7**
Buried deep in the heart of my soul.

G **D/A** **G/B** **C**
So se - cure that no pow - er can mine it away,

G **D7** **G**
While the years of e - ternity roll.

Copyright © 2015 by HAL LEONARD CORPORATION
International Copyright Secured All Rights Reserved

Chorus 2 *Repeat Chorus 1*

Verse 3

G D/A G/B C G
I am resting tonight in this wonderful peace,

A7 D7sus D7
Resting sweetly in Jesus' con - trol.

G D/A G/B C
For I'm kept from all dan - ger by night and by day,

G D7 G
And His glory is flooding my soul.

Chorus 3 *Repeat Chorus 1*

Verse 4

G D/A G/B C G
And me thinks when I rise to that city of peace,

A7 D7sus D7
Where the Author of peace I shall see,

G D/A G/B C
That one strain of the song which the ransomed will sing,

G D7 G
In that heavenly kingdom will be,

Chorus 4 *Repeat Chorus 1*

Verse 5

G D/A G/B C G
Ah, soul, are you here with - out comfort or rest,

A7 D7sus D7
Marching down the rough pathway of time?

G D/A G/B C
Make Jesus your friend ere the shadows grow dark,

G D7 G
O ac - cept of this peace so sub - lime.

Chorus 5 *Repeat Chorus 1*

Wondrous Love

Southern American Folk Hymn

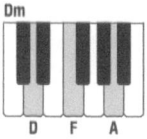

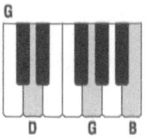

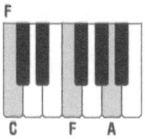

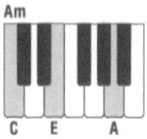

Verse 1

Dm G Dm F
What wondrous love is this,

Am Dm F Am
O my soul, O my soul,

F Am F
What wondrous love is this,

Am Dm
O my soul!

G Am Dm
What wondrous love is this

Am F Dm
That caused the Lord of bliss

G Dm F
To bear the dreadful curse

Am Dm Am
For my soul, for my soul,

F Am Dm
To bear the dreadful curse for my soul!

Copyright © 2015 by HAL LEONARD CORPORATION
International Copyright Secured All Rights Reserved

Verse 2

G Dm F
What wondrous love is this,

Am Dm F Am
O my soul, O my soul,

F Am F
What wondrous love is this,

Am Dm
O my soul!

G Am Dm
What wondrous love is this

Am F Dm
That caused the Lord of Life

G Dm F
To lay aside His crown

Am Dm Am
For my soul, for my soul,

F Am Dm
To lay aside His crown for my soul!

Verse 3

G Dm F
To God and to the Lamb

Am Dm F Am
I will sing, I will sing,

F Am F
To God and to the Lamb

Am Dm
I will sing.

G Am Dm
To God and to the Lamb

Am F Dm
Who is the Great I AM,

G Dm F
While millions join the theme,

Am Dm Am
I will sing, I will sing.

F Am Dm
While millions join the theme, I will sing!

Verse 4

G Dm F
And when from death I'm free,

Am Dm F Am
I'll sing on, I'll sing on,

F Am F
And when from death I'm free,

Am Dm
I'll sing on.

G Am Dm
And when from death I'm free,

Am F Dm
I'll sing and joyful be,

G Dm F
And through eterni - ty

Am Dm Am
I'll sing on, I'll sing on,

F Am Dm
And through eterni - ty I'll sing on!

PIANO CHORD SONGBOOK

HAL LEONARD PROUDLY PRESENTS THE

Piano Chord Songbook Series

Play and sing your favorite songs with the Piano Chord Songbook series! These collections include lyrics and piano chord diagrams for dozens of popular hit songs. At 6" x 9", these portable songbooks will come in handy just about anywhere you want to play!

The Beatles A-I
100 of their hits starting with A-I, including: Across the Universe • All My Loving • Back in the U.S.S.R. • Dear Prudence • Good Day Sunshine • A Hard Day's Night • Here Comes the Sun • and more.
00312017 ..... $16.99

The Beatles J-Y
This second volume includes 100 more songs starting with the letters J-Y: Lady Madonna • Ob-La-Di, Ob-La-Da • Paperback Writer • Revolution • Ticket to Ride • Yellow Submarine • and more.
00312018 ..... $16.99

Gospel Hymns
80 gospel favorites, including: Amazing Grace • Blessed Assurance • His Eye Is on the Sparrow • I Love to Tell the Story • Just a Closer Walk with Thee • Rock of Ages • There Is a Balm in Gilead • Will the Circle Be Unbroken • and many more.
00150122 ..... $14.99

Billy Joel
60 of the piano man's best, including: And So It Goes • It's Still Rock and Roll to Me • Just the Way You Are • Keeping the Faith • My Life • Piano Man • She's Got a Way • Tell Her About It • Uptown Girl • You May Be Right • and more.
00113722 ..... $12.99

Elton John
60 hits from this piano icon, including: Bennie and the Jets • Goodbye Yellow Brick Road • Mona Lisas and Mad Hatters • Tiny Dancer • Your Song • and more.
00311960 ..... $12.99

Praise & Worship
80 songs, including: Above All • As the Deer • Days of Elijah • Here I Am to Worship • In Christ Alone • Mighty to Save • Revelation Song • Shout to the Lord • We Fall Down • and more.
00311976 ..... $12.99

Taylor Swift
40 tunes from this talented songwriter, including: Back to December • Dear John • Fearless • Fifteen • Hey Stephen • Love Story • Mean • Our Song • Speak Now • White Horse • You Belong with Me • and more.
00312094 ..... $14.99

Three Chord Songs
58 three-chord classic hits, including: Authority Song • Bad Case of Loving You • Bye Bye Love • Kansas City • La Bamba • Twist and Shout • and more.
00311814 ..... $12.99

0715

Visit Hal Leonard online at
www.halleonard.com

FOR MORE INFORMATION, SEE YOUR LOCAL MUSIC DEALER, OR WRITE TO:

7777 W. BLUEMOUND RD. P.O. BOX 13819 MILWAUKEE, WI 53213

The Best Sacred Collections for Piano

The Big Book of Hymns

An invaluable collection of 125 favorite hymns, including: All Hail the Power of Jesus' Name • Battle Hymn of the Republic • Blessed Assurance • For the Beauty of the Earth • Holy, Holy, Holy • It Is Well with My Soul • Just as I Am • A Mighty Fortress Is Our God • The Old Rugged Cross • Onward Christian Soldiers • Rock of Ages • Sweet By and By • What a Friend We Have in Jesus • Wondrous Love • and more.

00310510 P/V/G $17.95

The Best Gospel Songs Ever

80 of the best-loved gospel songs of all time: Amazing Grace • At Calvary • Because He Lives • Behold the Lamb • Daddy Sang Bass • His Eye Is on the Sparrow • His Name Is Wonderful • How Great Thou Art • I Saw the Light • I'll Fly Away • Just a Closer Walk with Thee • Just a Little Talk with Jesus • Mansion over the Hilltop • The Old Rugged Cross • Peace in the Valley • Will the Circle Be Unbroken • Wings of a Dove • more.

00310503 P/V/G $19.99

The Christian Children's Songbook

101 songs from Sunday School, all in appropriate keys for children's voices. Includes: Awesome God • The B-I-B-L-E • Clap Your Hands • Day by Day • He's Got the Whole World in His Hands • Jesus Loves Me • Let There Be Peace on Earth • This Little Light of Mine • more.

00310472 P/V/G $19.95

The Hymn Collection

arranged by Phillip Keveren

17 beloved hymns expertly and beautifully arranged for solo piano by Phillip Keveren. Includes: All Hail the Power of Jesus' Name • I Love to Tell the Story • I Surrender All • I've Got Peace Like a River • Were You There? • and more.

00311071 Piano Solo $11.95

Hymn Duets

arranged by Phillip Keveren

Includes lovely duet arrangements of: All Creatures of Our God and King • I Surrender All • It Is Well with My Soul • O Sacred Head, Now Wounded • Praise to the Lord, The Almighty • Rejoice, The Lord Is King • and more.

00311544 Piano Duet $10.95

Hymn Medleys

arranged by Phillip Keveren

Great medleys resonate with the human spirit, as do the truths in these moving hymns. Here Phillip Keveren combines 24 timeless favorites into eight lovely medleys for solo piano.

00311349 Piano Solo $10.95

Hymns for Two

arranged by Carol Klose

12 piano duet arrangements of favorite hymns: Amazing Grace • Be Thou My Vision • Crown Him with Many Crowns • Fairest Lord Jesus • Holy, Holy, Holy • I Need Thee Every Hour • O Worship the King • What a Friend We Have in Jesus • and more.

00290544 Piano Duet $10.99

Ragtime Gospel Hymns

arranged by Steven Tedesco

15 traditional gospel hymns, including: At Calvary • Footsteps of Jesus • Just a Closer Walk with Thee • Leaning on the Everlasting Arms • What a Friend We Have in Jesus • When We All Get to Heaven • and more.

00311763 Piano Solo $8.95

Seasonal Sunday Solos for Piano

24 blended selections grouped by occasion. Includes: Breath of Heaven (Mary's Song) • Come, Ye Thankful People, Come • Do You Hear What I Hear • God of Our Fathers • In the Name of the Lord • Mary, Did You Know? • Mighty to Save • Spirit of the Living God • The Wonderful Cross • and more.

00311971 Piano Solo $14.99

Sunday Solos for Piano

30 blended selections, perfect for the church pianist. Songs include: All Hail the Power of Jesus' Name • Be Thou My Vision • Great Is the Lord • Here I Am to Worship • Majesty • Open the Eyes of My Heart • and many more.

00311272 Piano Solo $15.99

More Sunday Solos for Piano

A follow-up to *Sunday Solos for Piano*, this collection features 30 more blended selections perfect for the church pianist. Includes: Agnus Dei • Come, Thou Fount of Every Blessing • The Heart of Worship • How Great Thou Art • Immortal, Invisible • O Worship the King • Shout to the Lord • Thy Word • We Fall Down • and more.

00311864 Piano Solo $14.99

Even More Sunday Solos for Piano

30 blended selections, including: Ancient Words • Brethren, We Have Met to Worship • How Great Is Our God • Lead On, O King Eternal • Offering • Savior, Like a Shepherd Lead Us • We Bow Down • Worthy of Worship • and more.

00312098 Piano Solo $14.99

HAL•LEONARD® CORPORATION

7777 W. BLUEMOUND RD. P.O. BOX 13819 MILWAUKEE, WI 53213

www.halleonard.com

P/V/G = Piano/Vocal/Guitar arrangements.

Prices, contents and availability subject to change without notice.